TEXTUAL PRACTICE

GW01466207

VOLUME 1

NUMBER 1

SPRING 1987

Contents

Editorial

It is never a good time to start a new journal. Even so, 1987 seems unpropitious to a remarkable degree. The academic world in general feels itself to be under attack. The Humanities in particular feel marginalized and underfunded. Outwardly querulous, inwardly riven, they sense themselves to be hopelessly at odds with a culture which has long abandoned any recognition of the value of their role. Connoisseurs of the Unripe Time could be forgiven for regarding the present year as a vintage one, with the project represented by *Textual Practice* self-evidently foredoomed.

Yet there are signs that point in a different direction. Exactly ten years ago, the *New Accents* series made its initial contact with what could best be described as a diffused dissatisfaction with, and impulse for change in, an area centring on the study of literature. In practice, that area quickly turned out to include activities as apparently diverse as philosophy, history, sociology, cultural studies, communication studies, feminism, film and television studies. By now, aspects of that change have undeniably taken root and they manifest themselves in concrete terms on syllabuses the length and breadth of Britain and the United States.

Textual Practice represents a response to that continuing process, and to what might now be said to be its most clearly discernible shape and direction. In all the areas mentioned above, the effect of new theory, and the pondering of major social, historical and political issues it evokes, has been to establish and foster a fundamental and greatly extended notion of 'textuality': the perception, deriving from the study of literature, that a culture's significant activities involve a process which may fruitfully be conceived in terms of the production and consumption, the reading and writing of 'texts'.

Textual Practice aims to develop the implications of this concept across a whole spectrum of disciplines, practices and institutions, and to reflect and provide a platform for the many kinds of work already under way. Though the study of literary texts will be a central concern, received literary notions of 'textuality' will be critically challenged by the exploration of a range of semiotic systems.

Textual Practice will thus also seek to initiate and pursue interests in such areas as philosophy, law, politics, history, the history of science, feminism and cultural and media studies. These are spheres in which textual issues have always been crucially at stake, even though they have found themselves traditionally excluded from critical enquiry as we currently tend to think of it.

Textual Practice will explore this ground in an effort to challenge the boundaries that presently and misleadingly partition it. By means of articles, reviews, surveys, commentary and (let's hope) letters from its readers it will seek, quite simply, to explain, expand and enrich what is meant by the critical study of texts.

For if we live in a world in which texts of all kinds surround, penetrate and determine our lives, we need at the very least to know how they operate, to what end, and on behalf of whom. This may not be the best time to start a new journal. But there was never a time when one such as *Textual Practice* was more necessary.

Terence Hawkes

TERRY EAGLETON

The end of English

'It is my revolt against the English conventions, literary and otherwise, that is the main source of my talent,' James Joyce once told a friend.[1] In an old familiar paradox of English modernism, it is the colonized and dispossessed who shall inherit the literary earth. Sean Golden, in a brilliantly suggestive essay on this subject, sees the Irish and Americans who seized the commanding heights of 'English' literature earlier in the century as able to carry through this audacious feat of inverted imperialism precisely because they lacked those vested emotional interests in an English literary tradition which hamstrung the natives.[2] James, Conrad, Eliot, Pound, Yeats, Joyce and Beckett could approach indigenous English traditions from the outside, objectify and appropriate them for their own devious ends, estrange and inhabit English culture in a single act, as those reared within its settled pieties could not. Positioned as they were within essentially peripheral histories, such artists could view native English lineages less as a heritage to be protected than as an object to be problematized. A Joyce or an Eliot could ramble across the whole span of European literature, shameless *bricoleurs* liberated from the Oedipal constraints of a motherland.

When John Synge pulled off the improbable trick of seeming to write in English and Gaelic simultaneously, he was revealing the profoundly dialogical nature of all such modernism, which inflects its own interests in the tongue of another, inside and outside a hegemonic discourse at the same moment, the parasite which – as with the poker-faced conventionalism of Wilde and Shaw – merges into the very image of the host. The émigrés who turned themselves into Little Englanders (James, Conrad, Eliot) did so with all the studied self-consciousness of the *parvenu* anxiously seeking paternal approval, flamboyantly anglicized outsiders who became, self-parodically, more English than the English, hijacking their cultural baggage with all the insouciance of the circus clown who nips off with the suitcase the strong man has been struggling to lift. It was never easy to know whether Oscar Wilde, son (so they said) of the dirtiest man in Dublin, was flattering English high society with his effortless imitations or impudently sending them up.

The pact between modernism and colonialism in early twentieth-century England, today being repeated with a difference in Latin America, turns on a profound historical irony. If the Irish were partly liberated from the dead weight of English bourgeois tradition, free since the days of Laurence

Sterne to parody, subvert and disrupt, this was possible only because England over the centuries had stripped *them* of their native culture, thrown their national identity into dramatic crisis in a familiarly modernist way. Ireland became a devastated terrain in which everything had to be invented from scratch – in which, as with the brazenly opportunist narrators of Samuel Beckett's fiction, you made it up as you went along, turning political oppression to artistic advantage. Hence the later Yeats's solemn fiction of a homogeneous Anglo-Irish lineage, scooping the ill-assorted Swift, Goldsmith, Berkeley and Burke into portentous mythical continuity. Hence Eliot's habit of knocking off what seemed convenient from the European past, then piously consecrating this eclectic *mélange* of scraps and leavings with all the dignity of Tradition. 'Nothing is stable in this country,' wrote Joyce's brother Stanislaus; and it was exactly this sense of slippage and erasure, this chronic colonial incapacity to say who one was, which helped to nurture an Irish modernism at just the point where the realist, imperialist British were able to name themselves all too well. The effects of the empire striking back can still be felt today, in a British Isles whose finest poet is Irish, and whose major radical critic is Welsh.

'English literature' was the product of a Victorian imperial middle class, anxious to crystallize its spiritual identity in a material corpus of writing. No sooner had this discourse been refined to a point of maturity, however, than it was violently assailed by three structurally interrelated phenomena: the First World War, the explosion of modernism, and the mutation of the capitalist mode of production. All three phenomena are marked by an internationalism deeply at odds with the fostering of a national cultural formation. The First World War rocked those national securities to their foundation, at the same time as it lent increased impetus to the task of reinventing them as a refuge from ideological catastrophe. It is no accident that 'English', as moral discipline and spiritual balm, developed apace in post-war Cambridge, as a whole alternative identity for an exhausted imperial nation in accelerated decline. But, if English literary *criticism* takes root in this period, English *literature* does not. Major literary production shifts in large measure from the imperialist heartlands to the colonial or post-colonial periphery, leaving metropolitan criticism bereft of an appropriate contemporary object and bending it inexorably backwards, away from a despised and alien modernism to an imaginary native past. Modern English criticism, in other words, was *structurally* regressive from the outset, even as it sought to occupy the progressive role left open by its dismissal of the avant-garde. Hence the notorious ambiguities of *Scrutiny*, at once spiritual vanguard and reactionary rump, urgently responsive to the exigencies of the present at precisely the moment it pressed back into an idealized past.

In this contradictory situation, criticism confronts the unenviable destiny of becoming its own avant-garde, doubly estranged from its contemporary cultural moment in that the past it pits against the present is itself an idealized construct. *Scrutiny* became a displaced, distorted 'modernity', catching up in its vibrant, polemical, programmatic forms of cultural campaigning something of the pathbreaking zeal of the European avant-garde, while stoutly repelling most of the products of modernist Europe in its critical content. Caught precariously between imperialist hegemony and modernist revolt, English criticism was forced to counter the rebarbative realities of late capitalist culture with an *earlier* phase of bourgeois ideology: that of a liberal humanism already in the process of being historically superseded, on the defensive even in Matthew Arnold's day, a residual trace from a more buoyant, sanguine myth of bourgeois man. That this is still the major subjacent ideology of English studies half a century later is testimony both to the astonishing tenacity of that ideology, and to the increasing irrelevance of the entire project.

Scrutiny shared with modernism a certain marginal location, a resistance to the dominant metropolitan culture. If Ireland and New England were peripheral enclaves, then so in a different sense was Leavis's East Anglia. From both vantage-points, one could try to revaluate and reconstruct the dominant culture from the inside. The difference lay in the fact that what *Scrutiny* (and Bloomsbury) attempted – to oppose to both middle-class philistinism and upper-class frivolity the humane face of a liberal, non-conformist Englishness – was never a plausible tactic from the standpoint of the colonies. Joyce's *Ulysses* opens with the figure of the well-meaning English liberal Haines, who from Stephen Dedalus's viewpoint is of course no more than the acceptable face of Dublin Castle. H. G. Wells, recommending in a review that Joyce's *Portrait of the Artist as a Young Man* should be bought, read and locked up, whined that

> There is no discrimination in [its] hatred [of the British], there is no gleam of recognition that a considerable number of Englishmen have displayed a very earnest disposition to put matters right with Ireland . . . it is just hate, a cant cultivated to the pitch of monomania, an ungenerous violent direction of the mind.[3]

Joyce, of course, knew the stink of that Gladstonian earnestness about Ireland well enough – the well-meaning disposition of those who carried through the executions in Easter 1916.

From *Scrutiny*'s provincial standpoint, modernism and monopoly capitalism were akin in their cosmopolitan rootlessness, comrades in crime. It is a savage irony that its cult hero D. H. Lawrence spent his life tearing restlessly from one bit of the globe to another, a deracinated 'modern' if ever there was one. And *Scrutiny* was not, of course, wrong to discern a collusion between modernism and monopoly capitalism. For modernism's bold dissolution of national formations, that heady transgression of frontiers between both art forms and political states which led Philippe Sollers to describe *Finnegans Wake* as the greatest of anti-fascist novels, was, of course, made possible in part by the chronic nation-blindness of modern capitalism, which has no more respect than *The Waste Land* or the *Cantos* for regional particularism. The contradiction of such a system is that, in order to secure the political and ideological conditions for the international circulation of commodities, it needs to exploit exactly the national allegiances and identities which its economic activities constantly undermine.

In this sense, one can appreciate just what a desperate wager modernism must seem from a native nonconformist viewpoint: in seeking to challenge the oppressiveness of bourgeois nationhood, it must surrender itself inexorably to the rhythms of monopoly-capitalist internationalism, beginning, as Brecht said, from the 'bad new things' rather than the good old ones, permitting history to progress (as Marx said) by its bad side. For Leavis, there was a choice between being at home in your own language and being exiled in another's. But such a choice was not open to Joyce or Beckett, for whom one might as well be homeless in all languages as dispossessed in one's own. It is because the modernist colonials are exiled in their own speech, the tongue of the oppressor, that they can cast a cold eye on the notion of 'rootedness' – which is not to say that they did not have to pay, sometimes dearly, the price of a certain deeper deracination, as well as the cost of political isolation and aesthetic élitism. For Joyce and Beckett, as for Conrad before them, the paradigm case of the problematical nature of all discourse is to be disinherited in and by one's 'mother tongue'. Modernist cosmopolitanism, so to speak, merely universalizes the pain. One can trace this difficulty today in the poetry of Seamus Heaney, where a stubbornly specific regionalism (that of Catholic Derry) strives to articulate itself in a deftly cosmopolitan medium, in a linguistic pact constantly threatened with infidelity on both sides.

Since nobody actually lives absolved from all local allegiance, not even Joyce in Trieste or Pound in Rapallo, there is always an inevitably utopian moment in all such modernism – an assertive wager that one can be at home everywhere, in an equitable circulation of tongues, myths and identities of which the *Wake* is prototypical. And this, of course, is often enough compensation for the actual pains of exile. Those contemporary theories which would have us kick the referent and live euphorically on the inside of some great intertextual tangle of signs are, whether they know it or not, the appropriate coding of this real historical situation, and too often repress its actual misery. The utopic euphoria of such modernism corresponds in fact to an earlier moment of the twentieth-century capitalist mode of production, one which, despite Sollers's comment on the *Wake*, pre-dates the century's most virulent outbreak of nationalism, as well as the post-war consolidation of an international monopoly capitalism about which there seems little that is exhilarating. The cosmopolitan confidence of the early modernists has a different historical root: not only in the apparent promise of a more dynamic phase of capitalist technology, but in the more assertive international presence of its historical antagonist, the working class, which like the modernist artist knows no homeland. If art for the modernist writer was the name of that other, geographically unlocatable space where national identities crumbled, exploitation was its name for the world proletariat, and oppression for its subjugated groups and peoples.

British capitalism, however, had none of the restless dynamism which might have plausibly thrown up a futurism or constructivism. What attracted the 'Little Englander' literary émigrés to these shores, from James and Conrad to T. S. Eliot, was precisely the relatively settled nature of bourgeois hegemony, fruit of several centuries of imperialist domination abroad and class-collaborationism at home. Inertly traditionalist, replete with literary realism and liberal empiricism, English culture proved peculiarly resistant to the modernist experiment, just as for exactly the same reasons it inspired it by reaction in such writers as Joyce and Lawrence. England's closedness to modernism, which it 'exported' to the margins, meant on the one hand a welcome exclusion of subversive cultural forms. But it was at the same time a sign of capitalist stagnation and decline, and the ideology of 'Englishness' thrived on this backwardness. Shaken though it is in the early modernist period by severe class struggle, it is still at this point far from clear that England is finished – far from obvious that some refurbished 'nativism' *à la Scrutiny*, for all its regressive aspects, may not play some role in national reconsolidation. In such a context, modernism could be defused and domesticated, judiciously blended as in the later Eliot with a suitably Anglican tone and sensibility. Eliot could be aligned with Donne and Hopkins rather than with Mallarmé and Valéry; and it was the role of English criticism to effect such an alignment.

Besides, England still had at this point one powerful internationalist response to modernist cosmopolitanism: empire. If empire proved a breeding ground for modernism, as in the case of Ireland, it could also act as a bulwark for the mother country against it. English was a language in which one could be internationally at home, subsuming all regional particularities from Kerry to Kuala Lumpur, and thus resolving at a stroke the painful antithesis between parochialism on the one hand and global rootlessness on the other. Empire was England's secret weapon against a promiscuous modernism: the mere fact of the global reach of the English language was enough to buttress an indigenous culture otherwise grievously threatened with decline.

Englishness thus survived the modernist onslaught, which not long after the death of Lawrence had come to seem like a minor foreign aberration; but it then had to confront the much graver threat of the loss of empire itself. In the very enclave of Cambridge English in the critically crucial 1920s, *A Passage to India* was already presaging this catastrophe, ominously marking the limits of realist and liberal empiricist discourse, while quite unable itself to venture beyond them. The regional particularism so favoured by the Leavises returns with a vengeance in the middle decades of the century, rearing its head in the unpleasantly unfamiliar form of the various national liberation movements which detach one colonial society after another from British hegemony. The response of 'English' to this development would be the pathetic farce of 'Commonwealth literature'. 'English' begins to lose its global guarantee, and plunges its liberal humanist guardians into a severe dilemma. For, if that liberalism is restless with ruling-class imperial arrogance, its own belief in the centrality of the native was historically supported by just such an imperial system. The demise of *Scrutiny*, and the opening up of the major period of struggle against British imperialism, are historically coincident.

It is characteristic of what might loosely be called the modernist sensibility, from Baudelaire to T. S. Eliot, that the archaic and the innovative, the primeval and the modern, begin to enter into what Walter Benjamin would call 'shocking constellations' with one another, so that in the very act of 'making it new' one finds oneself excavating in recycled forms the eternally recurrent genealogies of a buried past. This uncanny convergence of the old and the new is nowhere more striking than in the curious parallelisms between colonialism and late capitalism, the pre- and post-industrial. What liberal humanism speaks up for, against the aesthetics of modernism, is the unitary subject, linear history, the self as agent, the world as knowable and totalizable – all ideological notions thrown into instant disorder by the colonial experience. A chronically backward colony like Joyce's Ireland lends itself to modernism as well as it does precisely because such notions are phenomenologically unworkable. In such conditions, the subject is less the strenuously self-mastering agent of its historical destiny than empty, powerless, without a name. Linear time, which is always, so to speak, on the side of Caesar, becomes cyclical, repetitive, untotalizable, denuded of tradition and teleology. The great unities of subject and object beloved of bourgeois idealist epistemology are inoperative from the outset, the object a blank, fragmented materiality sunk in the nausea of the quotidian, the subject a mere function of its circumstances, depthless and dispossessed. Meanwhile, altogether elsewhere, a classical bourgeois narrative of unified subjects, 'total' history and instantly intelligible signs conducts its triumphal existence, as the metropolitan fullness which drains the colonies dry.

What will be steadily eroded in the development of late capitalism, however, is precisely this apparently stable antithesis between colonial margin and metropolitan centre. For, as capitalism evolves beyond its great liberal-progressive epoch, it will come to seem as though the literature of modernist colonialism acted all along as the secret negative truth of the hegemony which produced it, prefiguring the final destiny of metropolitan society itself. As liberal capitalism yields ground to consumerism, it is as though a whole society undergoes the spiritual depletion and disinheritance previously reserved, with particular violence, for its meanest colonials. The margin shifts to the centre: now it is as though the very subjects of metropolitan capitalism are empty, dwindled, decentred, effects rather than agents, linear history struck vacuous by the ceaseless return of the commodity, cultural tradition brutally extirpated by the fetish of the Now. 'Primitive' mythology, repressed by the Enlightenment, returns with a vengeance: human life seems once more determined by great constant forces invisible to the naked eye, which shuffle around the contingent bits and pieces of reality in those gratuitous kaleidoscopic patterns we call 'change'. And just as the colonies seemed particularly hospitable to fantasy, to the dissolution of any stable reality in the great fracturings of repressed desire, so fantasy in the form of consumerism and the media now becomes structural to metropolitan society. Much of this, of course, was already evident in 'classical' modernism: what happens in the postmodern period is, first, that with the spread of consumerist capitalism these phenomena cease to be the artistic vision of an élite and penetrate more deeply into everyday life; and, second, that they become dissociated from the more positive, subversive, exhilarating impulses which earlier attended them. That positivity is once more 'exported': as all of this occurs within metropolitan society, the previously inert colonies gather strength in a striking historical inversion, begin to assert agency and fashion an intelligible history, translate dreams of freedom into political reality.

In the so-called postmodern condition, then, what was previously displaced to the margins returns to haunt the very centre: it is now not just Joyce's spiritually paralytic Dublin, but the stalely over-familiar global village of international monopoly capitalism, which revolves endlessly in the closed circuits of its mythologies. In this situation, 'English' begins to shed the last of its tattered credentials as any kind of ideologically plausible discourse. That discourse, I have argued, was seriously jeopardized by the First World War, but paradoxically consolidated by it. It was besieged almost instantly by modernism, but managed successfully to repel the alien invader. It had then to endure the loss of its global guarantee in the collapse of empire, but could still always turn back to a native tradition, constructing a literary lineage for itself from Hardy to Larkin in the manner of the young fogies of *PN Review*. What threatens it today is nothing less than the dissolution of its own subjacent ideology of liberal humanism, increasingly discredited by the later development of the very capitalism for which it was once so eloquent an apologist. The experiences of both modernism and colonialism were kept at bay, but in the latest historical irony now offer to respossess the metropolitan culture from inside in the shape of postmodernism. The fact that Donald Davie, one of the most vociferous spokespersons for post-imperial Little Englandism, actually emigrated to the USA some time ago is a nice irony: *actual* England is now, culturally speaking, pretty much like North America, and where you happen to be to launch your jeremiad is in that sense neither here nor there.

Perhaps the most minatory aspect of postmodernism for the ideology of English is its audio-visual character. This is not to espouse some glib mythology of the 'death of the novel', all of whose ritually issued obituary notices have proved remarkably premature. Those who regard writing as some charmingly archaic form no doubt have George Meredith rather than Robert Maxwell in mind. Nevertheless, it is a telling irony that contemporary literary theory has never been so obsessed with writing (admittedly in a suitably expanded sense of the term) in a cultural world where Rambo is only for a dwindling rump of us a French poet. The call for cultural studies, against some narrowly conceived literariness, is thus no more than a recognition of the inevitable. The mighty battles between parochial nativeness and modernist cosmopolitanism are being repeated in our own time, but this time as theory, which begins at Calais.

The terms of the conflict, however, are not quite the same as they were in the age of Joyce. At that time, as I have argued, it was still in some sense plausible for a native Englishness, buttressed by the reality of empire, to affirm itself, in a social order which had not yet witnessed the discrediting of liberal humanism as thoroughly as in our own. That ideology is still by no means to be underestimated: it remains powerfully entrenched in the academic institutions, and in the wider society still corresponds to some, though by no means all, the imperatives of late capitalism. But it is significant that in a period of capitalist crisis the guardians of English are now in danger of erasing the 'liberal' from the phrase 'liberal humanist'; and it is also significant that they are today quite incapable of anything like the robust, aggressive campaigning of *Scrutiny*, falling back instead on chauvinist gut reactions dressed up as spiritual intuitions. If Leavis did not see the need to tangle with 'theory', this in part reflected a certain confidence as well as a certain nervousness – the sense of a tangible cultural tradition being 'richly present', concretely demonstrable, and capable of enthusing a good number of acolytes. Today, the paucity of that intuitionism is painfully obvious, a clumsy, transparently rearguard action with nothing of the Leavisian *élan*. It is 'theory' that nowadays recruits the kind of committed, zealous young disciples that Leavis did in his day.

The end of empire, in short, has taken its toll: in a post-imperial, post-modernist culture, 'English', which for some time now has been living on like a headless chicken, has proved to be an increasingly unworkable discourse, if not in the cloistered universities, then most certainly in the inner-city schools. The struggle between that and 'theory' in some ways re-enacts the battles of modernism, but does so at a more explicitly political level. Some of the most vital arguments *within* contemporary literary theory, like the dissensions between 'high' modernism and the revolutionary avant-garde, concern the relative merits of a 'negative' and a 'positive' politics. It is possible to see Derrida, or even Paul de Man, as 'negatively' political in something like the way Adorno saw Beckett, or as Joyce saw his own writing. The modernist artists, however, were forced to devote too much time and energy to their own painful extrication from untenable cultural situations to address these political questions at all directly. Today, because we have less of such writing, or because much of it has been absorbed and defused, we have discovered a new terrain – theory, criticism – from which such questions can be launched. The current deconstruction of the very opposition between 'criticism' and 'creativity' is perhaps in one sense a reluctance to acknowledge the passing of 'high' modernism: they had the *Cantos*, we have Jonathan Culler. On the other hand, it involves a recognition that the subversive impulses of modernism can indeed migrate from domain to domain, are indeed portable across styles of discourse as across political frontiers. Whatever the historical losses, it is 'theory' which today attracts something of the virulent hostility once reserved for Eliot or Pound. The final discrediting of 'native Englishness' in a postmodernist epoch at least clarifies the issues at stake: as the material conditions which historically supported the ideology of 'English' have been gradually eroded, it is clearer than ever that the only conflict which finally matters is between the internationalism of late capitalist consumerism, and the internationalism of its political antagonist.

Wadham College, Oxford

NOTES

1 Ulrick O'Connor (ed.), *The James Joyce We Knew* (Cork, Mercier Press, 1967), p. 143.
2 Sean Golden, 'Post-traditional English literature: a polemic', *The Crane Bag Book of Irish Studies* (Dublin, Blackwater Press, 1982), pp. 427–38.
3 Quoted in ibid., p. 429.

LINDA HUTCHEON

Beginning to theorize postmodernism

Clearly, then, the time has come to theorize the term [post-
modernism], if not to define it, before it fades from awkward
neologism to derelict cliché without ever attaining to the
dignity of a cultural concept.

(Ihab Hassan)

Of all the terms bandied about in both current cultural theory and
contemporary writing on the arts, postmodernism must be the most over-
and under-defined. It is usually accompanied by a grand flourish of
negativized rhetoric: we hear of discontinuity, disruption, dislocation,
decentring, indeterminacy and anti-totalization. What all of these words
literally do (by their disavowing prefixes, *dis-, de-, in, anti-*) is incorporate
that which they aim to contest – as does, arguably, the term *postmodernism* itself. I point to this simple verbal fact in order to begin my
'theorizing' of the cultural enterprise to which we seem to have given such a
provocative label. First and foremost, I should like to argue, postmodernism is a contradictory phenomenon that uses and abuses, installs
and then subverts, the very concepts it challenges – be it in literature,
painting, sculpture, film, video, dance, television, music, philosophy,
aesthetic theory, psychoanalysis, linguistics or historiography. These are
some of the realms from which my 'theorizing' will proceed, and my
examples will always be specific, because what I want to avoid are those
polemical generalizations (often by those inimical to postmodernism –
Jameson 1984a, Eagleton 1985, Newman 1985) that leave us guessing
about just what it is that is being called postmodernist, though they are
never in doubt as to its undesirability. Some assume a generally accepted
'tacit definition' (Carmello 1983); others locate the beast by temporal
(after 1945? 1968? 1970? 1980?) or economic signposting (late capitalism).
But, in as pluralist and fragmented a culture as that of the Western world
today, such designations are not terribly useful if they intend to generalize
about all the vagaries of culture. After all, what does television's *Dallas*
have in common with the architecture of Ricardo Bofill? What does John
Cage's music share with a play (or film) like *Amadeus*?

In other words, postmodernism cannot simply be used as a synonym for the contemporary. And it does not really describe an international cultural phenomenon, for it is primarily European and American (North and South). Although the concept of *modernism* is largely an Anglo-American one (Suleiman 1986), this should not limit the poetics of *postmodernism* to that culture, especially since those who would argue that very stand are usually the ones to find room to sneak in the French *nouveau roman* (Wilde 1981; Brooke-Rose 1981; Lodge 1977). And almost everyone (e.g. Barth 1980) wants to be sure to include what Severo Sarduy (1974) has labelled not postmodernist but 'neo-baroque', in a Spanish culture where 'modernism' has a rather different meaning.

I offer instead, then, a specific, if polemical start from which to operate as a cultural activity that can be discerned in most art forms and many currents of thought today, what I want to call postmodernism is fundamentally contradictory, resolutely historical and inescapably political. Its contradictions may well be those of late capitalist society but, whatever the cause, these contradictions are certainly manifest in the important post-modern concept of 'the presence of the past'. This was the title given to the 1980 Venice Biennale which marked the institutional recognition of post-modernism in architecture. Italian architect Paolo Portoghesi's (1983) analysis of the twenty façades of the 'Strada Novissima' – whose very newness lay paradoxically in its historical parody – shows how architecture has been rethinking modernism's purist break with history. This is not a nostalgic return; it is a critical revisiting, an ironic dialogue with the past of both art and society, a recalling of a critically shared vocabulary of architectural forms. 'The past whose presence we claim is not a golden age to be recuperated,' argues Portoghesi (1983, p. 26). Its aesthetic forms and its social formations are problematized by critical reflection. The same is true of the postmodernist rethinking of figurative painting in art and historical narrative in fiction and poetry: it is always a critical reworking, never a nostalgic 'return'. Herein lies the governing role of irony in post-modernism. Stanley Tigerman's dialogue with history in his projects for family houses modelled on Raphael's Villa Madama is an ironic one: his miniaturization of the monumental forces is a rethinking of the social function of architecture – both then and now.

Because it is contradictory and works within the very systems it attempts to subvert, postmodernism can probably not be considered a new paradigm (even in some extension of the Kuhnian sense of the term). It has not replaced liberal humanism, even if it has seriously challenged it. It may mark, however, the site of the struggle of the emergence of something new. The manifestations in art of this struggle may be those undefinable, bizarre works like Terry Gilliam's film, *Brazil*. The postmodern ironic rethinking of history is here textualized in the many general parodic references to other movies: *A Clockwork Orange, 1984*, Gilliam's own *Time Bandits* and Monty Python sketches, and Japanese epics, to name but a few. The more specific parodic recalls range from *Star Wars'* Darth Vadar to the Odessa Steps sequence in Eisenstein's *Battleship Potemkin*. In *Brazil*, however, the baby carriage on the steps is replaced by a vacuum cleaner, and the result is to reduce epic tragedy to the bathos of the mechanical and debased (also achieved, of course, through the symbolic verbal suggestion of emptiness: 'vacuum' in that sense). Along with this ironic reworking of the history of film comes a temporal historical warp: the film is set, we are told, at 8.49 a.m. some time in the twentieth century. The décor does not help us identify the time more precisely. The fashions mix the absurdly futuristic with 1930s styling; an oddly old-fashioned and dingy setting belies the omnipresence of computers – though even they are not the sleekly designed creatures of today. Among the other typically postmodern contradictions in this movie is the coexistence of heterogeneous filmic genres: fantasy utopia and grim dystopia; absurd slapstick comedy and tragedy (the Tuttle/Buttle mix-up); the romantic adventure tale and the political documentary.

While all forms of contemporary art and thought have examples of this kind of postmodernist contradiction, here I (like most writers on the subject) shall be privileging the genre of novel, and one form in particular, a form that I want to label 'historiographic metafiction'. By this I mean those well-known and popular novels which are both intensely self-reflexive and yet lay claim to historical events and personages: *The French Lieutenant's Woman, Midnight's Children, Ragtime, Legs, G., Famous Last Words*. In most of the critical work on postmodernism, it is narrative – in fiction, history and theory – that has been the major focus of attention. Historiographic metafiction incorporates all three areas of concern: its theoretical self-awareness of history and fiction as human constructs (historio*graphic meta*fiction) is made the grounds for its rethinking and reworking of the forms and contents of the past. This kind of fiction has often been noticed, but its paradigmatic quality has been passed by: it is commonly labelled in terms of something else – for example, as 'midfiction' (Wilde 1981) or 'paramodernist' (Malmgren 1985). Such labelling is another mark of the inherent contradictoriness of historiographic metafiction, for it always works *within* conventions in order to subvert them. It is not pure metafiction, nor is it the same as the historical novel or the non-fictional novel. Gabriel García Márquez's *One Hundred Years of Solitude* has often been discussed in exactly the contradictory terms that I think define post-modernism. For example, Larry McCaffery sees it as both metafictionally self-reflexive and yet speaking to us powerfully about real political and historical realities: 'It has thus become a kind of model for the contemporary writer, being self-conscious about its literary heritage and about the limits of mimesis . . . but yet managing to reconnect its readers to the world outside the page' (1982, p. 264). What McCaffery here adds as almost an afterthought at the end of his book, *The Metafictional Muse*, is my starting point.

Most theorists of postmodernism who see it as a 'cultural dominant' (Jameson 1984a, p. 56) agree that it is characterized by the results of late capitalist dissolution of bourgeois hegemony and the development of mass culture (see Jameson 1984a (via Lefebvre 1968); Russell 1980; Egbert 1970; Calinescu 1977). I would agree and, in fact, argue that the increasing tendency towards uniformity in mass culture is one of the totalizing forces that postmodernism exists to challenge – challenge, but not deny. It does seek to assert difference, not homogeneous identity, but the very concept of difference could be said to entail a typically postmodernist contradiction: 'difference', unlike 'otherness', has no exact opposite against which to define itself. Thomas Pynchon allegorizes otherness in *Gravity's Rainbow* (1973) through the single, if anarchic, 'we-system' that exists as the counterforce of the totalizing 'They-system' (though it is also implicated in it). Postmodernist difference – or rather differences, in the plural – is always multiple and provisional.

Postmodernist culture, then, has a contradictory relationship to what we usually label the dominant or liberal humanist culture. It does not deny it, as some have asserted (Newman 1985, p. 42; Palmer 1977, p. 364). Instead, it contests it from within its own assumptions. Modernists like Eliot and Joyce have usually been seen as profoundly humanistic (Stern 1971, p. 26) in their paradoxical desire for stable aesthetic and moral values, even in the face of their realization of the inevitable absence of such universals. Postmodernism differs from this not in its humanistic contradictions but in the provisionality of its response to them: it refuses to posit any structure, or what Lyotard (1984a) calls master narrative – such as art or myth – which, for such modernists, would have been consolatory. It argues that such systems are indeed attractive, perhaps even necessary; but this does not make them any the less illusory. For Lyotard, post-modernism is characterized by exactly this kind of incredulity towards master and meta-narratives. Those who lament the 'loss of meaning' in the world or in art are really mourning the fact that knowledge is no longer primarily narrative knowledge of this kind (1984a, p. 26). This does not mean that knowledge somehow disappears. There is no radically new paradigm here, even if there is change.

It is no longer big news that the master narratives of bourgeois liberalism are under attack. There is a long history of many such sceptical sieges to positivism and humanism, and today's footsoldiers of theory – Foucault, Derrida, Habermas, Rorty, Baudrillard – follow in the footsteps of Nietzsche, Heidegger, Marx and Freud, to name but a few, in their challenges to the empiricist, rationalist, humanist assumptions of our cultural systems, including those of science (Graham 1982, p. 148; Toulmin 1972). Foucault's early rethinking of the history of ideas in terms of an 'archaeology' (*The Order of Things*, 1970; *The Archaeology of Knowledge*, 1972) that might stand outside the universalizing assumptions of humanism is one such attempt, whatever its obvious weaknesses. So is Derrida's more radical contesting of Cartesian and Platonic views of the mind as a system of closed meanings (see Harrison 1985, p. 6). In these terms, Habermas's work appears perhaps somewhat less radical in his desire to work from within the system of 'Enlightenment' rationality and yet manage to critique it at the same time. This is what Lyotard has attacked as just another totalizing narrative (1984b). And Jameson (1984b) has argued that both Lyotard and Habermas are resting their arguments on different but equally strong legitimizing 'narrative archetypes'.

This game of meta-narrative one-upmanship could go on and on, since arguably Jameson's Marxism leaves him vulnerable too. But this is not the point. What is important in all these internalized challenges to humanism is the interrogation of the notion of consensus. Whatever narratives or systems that once allowed us to think we could unproblematically define public agreement have now been questioned by the acknowledgement of differences – in theory and in artistic practice. In its most extreme formulation, the result is that consensus becomes the illusion of consensus, whether it be defined in terms of minority (educated, sensitive, élitist) or mass (commercial, popular, conventional) culture, for *both* are manifestations of late capitalist, bourgeois, informational, post-industrial society in which social reality is structured by discourses (in the plural) – or so postmodernism endeavours to teach.

What this means is that the familiar humanist separation of art and life (or human imagination and order versus chaos and disorder) no longer holds. Postmodernist contradictory art still installs that order, but it then uses it to demystify our everyday processes of structuring chaos, of imparting or assigning meaning (D'haen 1986, p. 225). For example, within a positivistic frame of reference, photographs could be accepted as neutral representations, as windows on the world. In the postmodernist photos of Heribert Berkert or Ger Dekkers, they still represent (for they cannot avoid reference), but what they represent is self-consciously shown to be highly filtered by the discursive and aesthetic assumptions of the camera holder (Davis 1977). While not wanting to go as far as Morse Peckham (1965) and argue that the arts are somehow 'biologically' necessary for social change, I would like to suggest that, in its very contradictions, postmodernist art might be able to dramatize and even provoke change from within. It is not that the modernist world was 'a world in need of mending' and the postmodernist one 'beyond repair' (Wilde 1981, p. 131). Postmodernism works to show that all repairs are human constructs, but that from that very fact they derive their value as well as their limitation. All repairs are both comforting and illusory. Postmodernist interrogations of humanist certainties live within this kind of contradiction.

Perhaps it is another inheritance from the sixties to believe that challenging and questioning are positive values (even if solutions to problems are not offered), for the knowledge derived from such enquiry may be the only possible condition of change. In the late 1950s, in *Mythologies*, Roland Barthes had prefigured this kind of thinking in his Brechtian challenges to all that is 'natural' or 'goes without saying' in our culture – that is, all that is considered universal and eternal, and therefore unchangeable. He suggested the need to question and demystify first, and then work for change. The sixties were the time of ideological formation for many of the postmodernist thinkers and artists of the eighties, and it is now that we can see the results of that formation.

Perhaps, as some have argued, the sixties themselves (i.e. at the time) produced no enduring innovation in aesthetics, but I would argue that they did provide the background, though not the definition, of postmodernism (cf. Bertens 1986, p. 17). They were crucial in developing a different concept of the possible function of art, one that would contest the 'Arnoldian' or humanist moral view with its élitist class bias (see Williams 1960, p. xiii). One of the functions of art in mass culture, argued Susan Sontag, would be to 'modify consciousness' (1967, p. 304). And many cultural commentators since have argued that the energies of the sixties have changed the framework and structure of how we consider art (e.g. Wasson 1974). The conservativism of the late seventies and eighties may have its impact when the thinkers and artists being formed now begin to produce their work (cf. McCaffery 1982), but to call Foucault or Lyotard a neo-conservative – as did Habermas (1983, p. 14) – is historically and ideologically inaccurate (see Calinescu 1986, p. 246; Giddens 1981, p. 17).

The political, social and intellectual experience of the sixties helped make it possible for postmodernism to be seen as what Kristeva calls 'writing-as-experience-of-limits' (1980, p. 137): limits of language, of subjectivity, of sexual identity and, we might also add, of systematization and uniformization. This interrogating (and even pushing) of limits has contributed to the 'crisis in legitimation' that Lyotard and Habermas see (differently) as part of the postmodern condition. It has certainly meant a rethinking and putting into question of the bases of our Western modes of thinking that we usually label, rather generally, liberal humanism.

What precisely, though, is being challenged? First of all, institutions have come under scrutiny: from the media to the university, from museums to theatres. The important contemporary debate about the margins and the boundaries of social and artistic conventions (see Culler 1983–4) is the result of a typically postmodernist transgressing of previously accepted limits: those of particular arts, of genres, of art itself. Rauschenberg's narrative (or discursive) work, *Rebus*, or Cy Twombly's series of Spenserian texts are indicative of the fruitful straddling of the borderline between the literary and visual arts. As early as 1969, Theodore Ziolkowski had noted that the 'new arts are so closely related that we cannot hide complacently behind the arbitrary walls of self-contained disciplines: poetics inevitably gives way to general aesthetics, considerations of the novel move easily to the film, while the new poetry often has more in common with contemporary music and art than with the poetry of the past' (1969, p. 113). The years since have only verified and intensified this perception. The borders between literary genres have become fluid: who can tell any more what the limits are between the novel and the short-story collection (Alice Munro's *Lives of Girls and Women*), the novel and the long poem (Michael Ondaatje's *Coming Through Slaughter*), the novel and autobiography (Maxine Hong Kingston's *China Men*), the novel and history (Salman Rushdie's *Shame*), the novel and biography (John Banville's *Kepler*)? But, in any of these examples, the conventions of the two genres are played off against each other; there is no simple, unproblematic merging. In Carlos Fuentes's *The Death of Artemio Cruz*, the title already points to the ironic inversion of biographical conventions: it is the death, not the life, that will be the focus. The subsequent narrative complications of three voices (first, second and third person) and three tenses (present, future, past) disseminate but also reassert (in a typically postmodernist way) the enunciative situation or discursive context of the work. The traditional verifying third-person, past-tense voice of History and realism is both installed and undercut by the others.

Clearly the most important boundaries crossed have been those between fiction and non-fiction and – by extension – between art and life. In the March 1986 issue of *Esquire* magazine, Jerzy Kosinski published a piece in the 'Documentary' section called 'Death in Cannes', a narrative of the last days and subsequent death of the French biologist Jacques Monod. Typically postmodernist, the text refuses the omniscience and omnipresence of the third person and engages instead in a dialogue between a narrative voice (which both is and is not Kosinski's) and a projected reader. Its viewpoint is avowedly limited, provisional, personal. However, it also works and plays with the conventions of both literary realism and journalistic facticity: the text is accompanied by photographs of the author and the subject. The commentary uses these photos to make us, as readers, aware of our expectations of both narrative and pictorial interpretation, including our naïve but common trust in the representational veracity of photography. One set of photos is introduced with the words 'I bet the smiling picture was taken last. I always bet on a happy ending' (1986, p. 82), but the subsequent prose section ends: 'look at the pictures if you must but . . . don't bet on them. Bet on the worth of a word' (p. 82). But we come to learn later that there are events – like Monod's death – that are beyond both words and pictures.

Kosinski calls this postmodernist form of writing 'autofiction': 'fiction' because all memory is fictionalizing; 'auto' because it is, for him, 'a literary genre, generous enough to let the author adopt the nature of his fictional protagonist – not the other way around' (p. 82). When he 'quotes' Monod, he tells the fictive and questioning reader that it is in his own '*autolingua* – the inner language of the storyteller' (p. 86). In his earlier novel, *Blind Date* (1977), Kosinski had used Monod's death and the text of his *Chance and Necessity* (1971) as structuring concepts in the novel: from both, he learned of our need to rid ourselves of illusions of totalizing explanations and systems of ethics. But it is not just this kind of historiographic metafiction that challenges the borders between life and art, that plays on the margins of genre. Painting and sculpture, for instance, come together with similar impact in some of the three-dimensional canvases of Robert Rauschenberg and Tom Wesselman (see D'haen 1986 and Owens 1980). And, of course, much has been made of the blurring of the distinctions between the discourses of theory and literature in the works of Jacques Derrida and Roland Barthes – or somewhat less fashionably, if no less provocatively, in some of the writing of Ihab Hassan (1975, 1980a) and Zulfikar Ghose (1983).

In addition to being 'borderline' enquiries, most of these postmodernist texts are also specifically parodic in their intertextual relation to the traditions and conventions of the genres involved. When Eliot recalled Dante or Virgil in *The Waste Land*, one sensed a kind of wishful call to continuity beneath the fragmented echoing. It is precisely this that is contested in postmodernist parody, where it is often ironic discontinuity that is revealed at the heart of continuity, difference at the heart of similarity (Hutcheon 1985). Parody is a perfect postmodernist form in some senses, for it paradoxically both incorporates and challenges that which it parodies. It also forces a reconsideration of the idea of origin or originality that is compatible with other postmodernist interrogations of liberal humanist assumptions. While Jameson (1983, pp. 114–19) sees this loss of the modernist unique, individual style as negative, as an imprisoning of the text in the past through pastiche, it has been seen by postmodernist *artists* as a liberating challenge to a definition of subjectivity and creativity that has ignored the role of history in art and thought. On Rauschenberg's use of reproduction and parody in his work, Douglas Crimp writes: 'The fiction of the creating subject gives way to the frank confiscation, quotation, excerptation, accumulation and repetition of already existing images. Notions of originality, authenticity and presence . . . are undermined' (1983, p. 53). The same is true of the fiction of John Fowles or the music of George Rochberg. As Foucault noted, the concepts of subjective consciousness and continuity that are now being questioned are tied up with an entire set of ideas that have been dominant in our culture until now: 'the point of creation, the unity of a work, of a period, of a theme . . . the mark of originality and the infinite wealth of hidden meanings' (1972, p. 230).

Another consequence of this far-reaching postmodernist enquiry into the nature of subjectivity (or of the self) is the frequent challenge to traditional notions of perspective, especially in narrative and painting. The perceiving subject is no longer assumed to be a coherent, meaning-generating entity. Narrators in fiction become either disconcertingly multiple and hard to locate (as in D. M. Thomas's *The White Hotel*) or resolutely provisional and limited – often undermining their own seeming omniscience (as in Salman Rushdie's *Midnight's Children*). In Charles Russell's terms, with postmodernism we start to encounter and are challenged by 'an art of shifting perspective, of double self-consciousness, of local and extended meaning' (1980, p. 192).

As Foucault and others have suggested, linked to this contesting of the unified and coherent self is a more general questioning of *any* totalizing or homogenizing system. Provisionality and heterogeneity contaminate any neat attempts at unifying coherence – formal or thematic. Historical and narrative continuity and closure are contested, but again from within. The teleology of art forms – from fiction to music – is both suggested and transformed. The centre no longer completely holds; from the decentred perspective, the 'marginal' and the ex-centric (be it in race, gender or ethnicity) take on new significance in the light of the implied recognition that our culture is not really the homogeneous monolith (i.e. male, white,

Western) we might have assumed. The concept of alienated otherness (based on binary oppositions that conceal hierarchies) gives way, as I have argued, to that of differences: to the assertion not of centralized sameness but of decentralized community – another postmodernist paradox. The local and the regional are stressed in the face of mass culture and a kind of vast global informational village that McLuhan could only have dreamed of. Culture (with a capital C and in the singular) has become cultures (uncapitalized and plural), as documented at length by our social scientists. And this appears to be happening in spite of – and, I would argue, maybe even because of – the homogenizing impulse of the consumer society of late capitalism – yet another postmodernist contradiction. In attempting to define what he called the 'trans-avant-garde', the Italian art critic Achille Bonito Oliva found he had to talk of differences as much as similarities from country to country (1984, pp. 71–3): it would seem that the 'presence of the past' depends on the local and culture-specific nature of each past.

In this sort of context, different kinds of texts will take on value – the ones that operate what Derrida calls 'breaches or infractions' – for it is they that can lead us to suspect the very concept of 'art' (1981, p. 69). In Derrida's words, such artistic practices seem 'to mark and to organize a structure of resistance to the philosophical conceptuality that allegedly dominated and comprehended them, whether directly, or whether through categories derived from this philosophical fund, the categories of esthetics, rhetoric, or traditional criticism' (p. 69). Of course, Derrida's own texts belong solely to neither philosophical nor literary discourse, though they partake of both in a deliberately self-reflexive and contradictory (post-modern) manner.

Derrida's constant self-consciousness about the status of his own discourse raises another question that must be faced by anyone – like myself – writing on postmodernism. From what position does one 'theorize' (even self-consciously) a disparate, contradictory, multivalent, current cultural phenomenon? Stanley Fish (1986) has wittily pointed out the 'anti-foundationalist' paradox that I too find myself in when I comment on the importance of Derrida's critical self-consciousness. In Fish's ironic terms: 'Ye shall know that truth is not what it seems and *that* truth shall set you free.' Barthes, of course, had seen the same danger earlier as he watched demystification become part of the *doxa* (1977, p. 166). Similarly Christopher Norris has noted that, in textualizing all forms of knowledge, deconstruction theory often, in its very unmasking of rhetorical strategies, still itself lays claim to the status of 'theoretical knowledge' (1985, p. 22). Most postmodernist theory, however, realizes this paradox or contradiction. Rorty, Baudrillard, Foucault, Lyotard and others seem to imply that any knowledge cannot escape complicity with meta-narratives, with the fictions that render possible any claim to 'truth', however provisional. What they add, however, is that *no* narrative can be a natural 'master' narrative; there are no natural hierarchies, only those we construct. It is this kind of self-implicating questioning that should allow postmodernist theory to challenge narratives that do presume to 'master' status, without necessarily assuming that status for itself.

Postmodernist art similarly asserts and then deliberately undermines such principles as value, order, meaning, control and identity (Russell 1985, p. 247) that have been the basic premises of bourgeois liberalism. Those humanistic principles are still operative in our culture, but for many they are no longer seen as eternal and unchallengeable. The contradictions of both postmodernist theory and practice are positioned within the system and yet work to allow its premises to be seen as fictions or as ideological structures. This does not necessarily destroy their 'truth' value, but it does define the conditions of that 'truth'. Such a process reveals rather than conceals the tracks of the signifying systems that constitute our world – that is, systems constructed by us in answer to our needs. However important these systems are, they are not natural, given or universal. The very limitations imposed by the postmodern view are also perhaps ways of opening new doors: perhaps now we can better study the interrelations of social, aesthetic, philosophical and ideological constructs. In order to do so, postmodernist critique must acknowledge its own position as an ideological one (Newman 1985, p. 60). I think the formal and thematic contradictions of postmodernist art and theory work to do just that: to call attention both to what is being contested and what is being offered as a critical response to that, and to do so in a self-aware way that admits its own provisionality.

In writing about these postmodernist contradictions, then, I clearly would not want to fall into the trap of suggesting any 'transcendental identity' (Radhakrishnan 1983, p. 33) or essence for postmodernism. I see it as an ongoing cultural process or activity, and I think that what we need, more than a fixed and fixing definition, is a 'poetics', an open, ever-changing theoretical structure by which to order both our cultural knowledge and our critical procedures. This would not be a poetics in the structuralist sense of the word, but would go beyond the study of literary discourse to the study of cultural practice and theory. As Tzvetan Todorov realized in a later expanding and translating of his 1968 *Introduction to Poetics*: 'Literature is inconceivable outside a typology of discourses' (1981, p. 71). Art and theory about art (and culture) should both be part of a poetics of postmodernism. Richard Rorty has posited the existence of 'poetic' moments 'as occurring periodically in many different areas of culture – science, philosophy, painting and politics, as well as the lyric and the drama' (1984, p. 4). But this is no coincidental moment; it is made, not found. As Rorty explains:

> it is a mistake to think that Derrida, or anybody else, 'recognized' problems about the nature of textuality or writing which had been ignored by the tradition. What he did was to think up ways of speaking which made old ways of speaking optional, and thus more or less dubious. (Rorty 1984, p. 23n.)

It is both a way of speaking – a discourse – and a cultural process that a poetics would seek to articulate.

A poetics of postmodernism would not posit any relation of causality or identity among the arts or between art and theory. It would merely offer, as provisional hypotheses, perceived overlappings of concern, here specifically with regard to the contradictions of postmodernism. It would not be a matter of reading literature as continuous with theory, nor seeing literary theory as an imperialistic intellectual practice (White 1978, p. 261). The interaction of theory and practice in postmodernism is a complex one of shared responses to common provocations. There are also, of course, many postmodernist artists who double as theorists – Eco, Lodge, Bradbury, Barth – though they have rarely become the major theorists or apologists of their own work as the *nouveaux romanciers* (from Robbe-Grillet to Ricardou) and surfictionists (Federman and Sukenick especially) have tended to do. What a poetics of postmodernism would articulate is less the theories of Eco in relation to *The Name of the Rose* than the overlappings of concern between, for instance, the contradictory form of the writing of theory in Lyotard's *Le Différend* (1983) and that of a novel like Peter Ackroyd's *Hawksmoor* (1985). Their sequentially ordered sections are equally disrupted by a particularly dense network of interconnections and intertexts, and each enacts or performs, as well as theorizes, the paradoxes of continuity and disconnection, of totalizing interpretation and the impossibility of final meaning. In Lyotard's own words:

> A postmodern artist or writer is in the position of a philosopher: the text he writes, the work he produces are not in principle governed by preestablished rules, and they cannot be judged according to a determining judgment, by applying familiar categories to the text or to the work. Those rules and categories are what the work of art itself is looking for. (1984b, p. 81)

Jameson has listed 'theoretical discourse' among the manifestations of postmodernism (1983, p. 112), and this would include not just the obvious post-structuralist philosophical and literary theory but also analytic philosophy, psychoanalysis, linguistics, historiography, sociology and other areas. Recently critics have begun to notice the similarities of concern between various kinds of theory and current literary discourse, sometimes to condemn (Newman 1985, p. 118), sometimes merely to describe (Hassan 1986). With novels like Ian Watson's *The Embedding* around, it is not surprising that the link would be made. I do not at all think, however, that this has contributed to any 'inflation of discourse' at the expense of historical contextualization (Newman 1985, p. 10), primarily because historiography is itself taking part in what LaCapra has called a 'reconceptualization of culture in terms of collective discourses' (1985, p. 46). By this he does not mean to imply that historians no longer concern themselves with 'archivally based documentary realism', but only that, within the discipline of history, there is also a growing concern with redefining intellectual history as 'the study of social meaning as historically constituted' (p. 46; see too White 1973, 1980, 1981, 1984). This is exactly what historiographic metafiction is doing: Graham Swift's *Waterland*, Rudy Wiebe's *The Temptations of Big Bear*, Ian Watson's *Chekhov's Journey*.

In the past, history has often been used in criticism of the novel as a kind of model of the realistic pole of representation. Postmodernist fiction problematizes this model to query the relation of both history to reality and reality to language. In Lionel Gossman's terms:

Modern history and modern literature [I would say *post*modern in both cases] have both rejected the ideal of representation that dominated them for so long. Both now conceive of their work as exploration, testing, creation of new meanings, rather than as disclosure or revelation of meanings already in some sense 'there', but not immediately perceptible. (1978, pp. 38–9)

The view that postmodernism relegates history to 'the dustbin of an obsolete episteme, arguing gleefully that history does not exist except as text' (Huyssen 1981, p. 35), is simply wrong. History is not made obsolete; it is, however, being rethought – as a human construct. And, in arguing that *history* does not exist except as text, it does not stupidly and 'gleefully' deny that the *past* existed, but only that its accessibility to us now is entirely conditioned by textuality. We cannot know the past except through its texts: its documents, its evidence, even its eye-witness accounts are *texts*. And postmodernist novels – *The Scorched-Wood People, Flaubert's Parrot, Antichthon, The White Hotel* – teach us about both this fact and its consequences.

Along with the obvious and much publicized case of postmodern architecture (Jencks 1977, 1980a, 1980b), it has been (American) black and (general) feminist theory and practice that have been particularly important in this postmodernist refocusing on historicity, both formally (largely through parodic intertextuality) and thematically. Works like Ishmael Reed's *Mumbo Jumbo*, Maxine Hong Kingston's *China Men* and Gayl Jones's *Corregidora* have gone far to expose – very self-reflexively – the myth- or illusion-making tendencies of historiography. They have also linked racial and/or gender difference to questions of discourse and of authority and power that are at the heart of the postmodernist enterprise in general and, in particular, of both black theory and feminism. All are theoretical discourses that have their roots in a reflection on actual praxis and continue to derive their critical force from their conjunction with that social and aesthetic practice (on feminism, see de Lauretis 1984, p. 184). It is true that, as Susan Suleiman (1986, p. 268, n. 12) acutely noted, literary discussions of postmodernism often appear to exclude the work of women (and, one might add, often of blacks as well), even though female (and black) explorations of narrative and linguistic form have been among the most contesting and radical. Certainly women and American black artists' use of parody to challenge the male white tradition from within, their use of irony to implicate and yet to critique, is distinctly paradoxical and postmodernist. Both black and feminist thought have shown how it is possible to move theory out of the ivory tower and into the larger world of social praxis, as theorists like Said (1983) have been advocating. Arguably, women have helped develop the postmodern valuing of the margins and the ex-centric as a way out of the power problematic of centres and of male/female oppositions (Kamuf 1982). Certainly Susan Swan's *The Biggest Modern Woman of the World*, a biographical metafiction about a real (and, by definition, ex-centric) giantess, would suggest precisely this in its opposition to what the protagonist sees as 'emblem fatigue': 'an affliction peculiar to giants [or women or blacks or ethnic minorities] who are always having to shoulder giant expectations from normal folk' (Swan 1983, p. 139).

There are other works which have come close to articulating the kind of poetics I think we need, though all offer a somewhat more limited version. But they too have investigated the overlappings of concern between current philosophical and literary theory and practice. Evan Watkins's *The Critical Act: Criticism and Community* (1978) aims to derive a theory of literature that can 'elicit from recent poetry in particular the means of talking about and talking back to developments in theory' (p. x). His model, however, is one of 'dialectical reciprocity', which often implies a causal relationship (p. 12) that the sort of poetics I envisage would avoid.

David Carroll's fine study, *The Subject in Question: The Languages of Theory and the Strategies of Fiction* (1982), is somewhat more limited than a general poetics of postmodernism would be, for it focuses on aporias and contradictions specifically in the work of Jacques Derrida and Claude Simon in order to study the limitations of both theory and fiction in examining the problem of history – limitations that are made evident by the confrontation of theory with practice. As I see it, however, a poetics would not seek to place itself in a position *between* theory and practice (Carroll 1982, p. 2) on the question of history, so much as in a position *within* both. A work like Peter Uwe Hohendahl's *The Institution of Criticism* (1982), while limited to the German context, is useful here in showing the kind of question that a poetics placed within both theory and practice must ask, especially regarding the norms and standards of *criticism*: the autonomous institution that mediates theory and practice in the field of literary studies.

Allen Thiher's *Words in Reflection: Modern Language Theory and Postmodern Fiction* (1984) comes closest to defining a general poetics, in that it studies some current theories, together with contemporary literary practice, in order to show what he feels to be a major 'displacement in the way we think and, perhaps more important, write the past' (p. 189). However, this lucid and thorough study limits itself to modern language theory and linguistically self-reflexive metafiction and posits a kind of influence model (of theory over fiction) that a poetics of postmodernism would not be willing to do. Rather than separate theory from practice, it would seek to integrate them and would organize itself around issues (representation, textuality, subjectivity, ideology, and so on) which both theory and art problematize and continually reformulate in paradoxical terms.

First, however, any poetics of postmodernism should come to terms with the immense amount of material that has already been written on the subject of postmodernism in all fields. The debate invariably begins over the meaning of the prefix, 'post-' – a four-letter word if ever there was one. Does it have as negative a ring of supersession and rejection as many contend (Barth 1980)? I would argue that, as is most clear perhaps in postmodern architecture, the 'Post Position' (Culler 1982, p. 81) signals its contradictory dependence on and independence from that which temporally preceded it and which literally made it possible. Postmodernism's relation to modernism is, therefore, typically contradictory. It marks neither a simple and radical break from it nor a straightforward continuity with it: it is both and neither. And this would be the case in aesthetic, philosophical or ideological terms.

Of the many arguments mounted on either side of the modernist/postmodernist debate, let me here consider only one in detail, a recent and influential one: that of Terry Eagleton in his 1985 article, 'Capitalism, modernism and postmodernism'. In fact, much of what is offered here is repeated in other theorizing on postmodernism. Like many before him (both defenders like Lyotard and detractors like Jameson), Eagleton separates practice and theory, choosing to argue only in abstract theoretical terms and seeming almost deliberately to avoid mention of exactly what kind of aesthetic practice is actually being talked about. This strategy, however clever and certainly convenient, leads only to endless confusion. My first response to his article, for instance, was that from the descriptive theorizing alone, Eagleton, like Jameson, must mean something quite different from what I do by postmodernism in art. Yet they both make passing references to architecture, and so I suppose I must presume, though I cannot prove it from their texts, that we are all indeed talking of the same kind of artistic manifestation. And so I shall proceed on that assumption. (I should also note that I find it ironic that, like Jameson, Eagleton finds himself in the same hostile position *vis-à-vis* postmodernism as Lukács had been *vis-à-vis* modernism, but that Eagleton looks to precisely what Lukács had denigrated for his set of valid norms and values: postmodernism becomes a 'sick joke' or parody of modernism (Eagleton 1985, p. 60).)

I want to look at each of Eagleton's eight major points in the light of the postmodernist artistic practice I have been discussing, for I think that his absolutist binary thinking – which makes postmodernism into the negative and opposite of modernism – denies much of the complexity of that art. His theory is neat, but maybe too neat. For example, can the historical and discursive contextualizing of Doctorow's *Ragtime* really be considered to be dehistoricized and devoid of historical memory? It may alter received historical opinion, but it does not evade the notions of historicity or historical determination. Is the highly individualized and problematic voice of Saleem Sinai in *Midnight's Children* really to be dubbed 'depthless' and 'without style'? Is that novel (or are Coover's *The Public Burning* or Doctorow's *The Book of Daniel*) seriously to be labelled as empty of political content? Yet Eagleton asserts all of this – minus the examples – as defining what he calls postmodernism (p. 61).

I would again ask: in Findley's *Famous Last Words*, does the obvious 'performativity' of the text really 'replace truth' (p. 63), or does it, rather, question *whose* notion of truth gains power and authority over others' and then examine the process of how it does so? The Brechtian involvement of the reader – both textualized (Quinn) and extratextual (us) – is something Eagleton appears to approve of in the modernist 'revolutionary' avant-garde. But it is also a very postmodernist strategy, and here leads to the acknowledgement, not of truth, but of truths in the plural – truths that are socially, ideologically and historically conditioned. Eagleton sees that postmodernism dissolves modernist boundaries, but regards this as negative, an act of becoming 'coextensive with commodified life itself' (p. 68). However, historiographic metafiction like Puig's *Kiss of the Spider Woman* works precisely to combat any aestheticist fetishing of art by *refusing* to bracket exactly what Eagleton wants to see put *back* into art: 'the referent or real historical world' (p. 67). What such fiction also does, though, is problematize both the nature of the referent and its relation to the real, historical world by its paradoxical combination of metafictional self-reflexivity with historical subject matter. How, then, could Cortázar's *A Manual for Manuel* be reduced to a celebration of 'kitsch' (p. 68) Is all art that introduces non-high forms (journalism or the spy story) by definition kitsch? What Eagleton (like Jameson (1984a) before him) seems to ignore is the subversive potential of irony, parody and humour in contesting the universalizing pretensions of 'serious' art.

Eagleton broadens the scope of his attack on postmodernism by describing it as 'confidently post-metaphysical' (p. 70). The one thing which the provisional, contradictory postmodernist enterprise is *not* is 'confidently' anything. A novel like Banville's *Doctor Copernicus* does not confidently accept that things are things, as Eagleton asserts. Its entire formal and thematic energy is founded in its philosophical problematizing of the nature of reference, of the relation of word to thing, of discourse to experience. Postmodernist texts like *The White Hotel* or *Kepler* do not confidently disintegrate and banish the humanist subject either, though Eagleton says that postmodernism (in his theoretical terms) does. They *do* disturb humanist certainties about the nature of the self and of the role of consciousness and Cartesian reason (or positivistic science), but they do so by inscribing that subjectivity and only then contesting it.

I have deliberately discussed each of Eagleton's eight points in terms of specific examples in order to illustrate the dangers of separating neat theory from messy practice. A poetics of postmodernism must deal with *both* and can theorize only on the basis of all the forms of postmodernist discourse available to it. The constant complaint either that postmodernism is ahistorical or, if it uses history, that it does so in a naïve and nostalgic way, just will not stand up in the light of actual novels such as those listed above or films like *Crossroads* or *Zelig*. What starts to look naïve, by contrast, is the reductive belief that any recall of the past must, by definition, be sentimental nostalgia or antiquarianism. What postmodernism does, as its very name suggests, is confront and contest any modernist discarding *or* recuperating of the past in the name of the future. It suggests no search for transcendent, timeless meaning but rather a re-evaluation of, and a dialogue with the past in the light of the present. We could call this, once again, 'the presence of the past' or perhaps its 'present-ification' (Hassan 1983). It does not deny the *existence* of the past; it does question whether we can ever *know* that past other than through its textualized remains.

These constant binary oppositions set up in the writing on post-modernism – between past and present, modern and postmodern, and so on – should probably be called into question, if only because, like the rhetoric of rupture (*dis*continuity, *de*centring, etc.), *post*modernism literally constitutes its own paradoxical identity, and does so in an uneasy, contradictory relationship of constant slippage. So much that has been written on this subject has physically taken the form of opposing columns, usually labelled 'modernist versus postmodernist' (see Hassan 1975, 1980b; cf. Lethen 1986, pp. 235–6) – a structure that denies the mixed, plural and contradictory nature of the postmodernist enterprise.

Whether this complexity is a result of our particularly contradictory age, caught between 'myths of totality' and 'ideologies of fracture' (Hassan 1980a, p. 191), is another question. Surely many ages could be so described. Whatever the cause, a poetics of postmodernism should try to come to grips with some of the obvious paradoxes in both theory and practice. Let me offer a few more examples: one would be the contradiction of a (textual) self-referentiality that is constantly confronted with (textual) discursive contextualizing, especially when it is done in such a way that the self-reflexivity inevitably moves toward surrounding discourses, as in the case of historiographic metafiction. Another major contradiction to be faced would be the irony of Lyotard's (1984a) obviously meta-narrative theory of postmodernism's incredulity to meta-narrative (see Lacoue-Labarthe 1984) or of Foucault's early anti-totalizing epistemic totalizations. These are typically paradoxical: they are the masterful denials of mastery, the cohesive attacks on cohesion, that characterize postmodernist theory. Similarly, historiographic metafiction – like postmodernist painting, sculpture and photography – inscribes and then subverts its mimetic engagement with the world. It does not reject it (Graff 1979); nor does it merely accept it (Butler 1980, p. 93; Wilde 1981, p. 170). But it does irrevocably change any simple notions of realism or reference, by confronting the discourse of art with the discourse of history.

A further postmodernist paradox that this particular kind of fiction enacts is to be found in its bridging of the gap between élite and popular art, a gap which mass culture has perhaps broadened. Many have noted postmodernism's attraction to popular art forms (Fiedler 1975) such as the detective story (Fowles's *A Maggot*) or the western (Doctorow's *Welcome* to *Hard Times* or Berger's *Little Big Man*). But what has not been dealt with is the paradox that novels like *The French Lieutenant's Woman* or *The Name of the Rose* themselves are both popular bestsellers and objects of intense academic study. I would argue that, as typically postmodernist contradictory texts, novels like these parodically use and abuse the conventions of both popular and élite literature, and do so in such a way that they can actually *use* the invasive culture industry to challenge its own commodification processes from within. If élitist culture has indeed been fragmented into specialist disciplines, as many have argued, then hybrid novels like these work both to address and to subvert that fragmentation through their pluralizing recourse to the discourses of history, sociology, theology, political science, economics, philosophy, semiotics, literature, literary criticism, and so on. Historiographic metafiction clearly acknowledges that postmodernism operates in a complex institutional and discursive network of élite, official, mass and popular cultures. Postmodernism may not offer any final answers, but perhaps it can begin to ask questions that may eventually lead to answers of some kind.

Unresolved paradoxes may be unsatisfying to those in need of absolute and final answers, but to postmodernist thinkers and artists they have been the source of intellectual energy which has provoked new articulations of the postmodern condition. Despite the obvious danger, they do not appear to have brought on what LaCapra has called a 'lemming-like fascination for discursive impasses' (1985, p. 141) which might threaten to undermine *any* working concept of 'theorizing'. The model of contradictions offered here – while admittedly only another model – would hope to open up any poetics of postmodernism to plural, contestatory elements without necessarily reducing or recuperating them. In order to try to avoid the tempting trap of co-option, it is necessary to acknowledge the fact that such a position is itself an ideology, one that is profoundly implicated in that which it seeks to theorize. We cannot exempt our own 'discriminating scholarly discourse', as Douwe Fokkema would like (1986, p. 2), for it too is as institutionalized as the fiction or the painting or the philosophy or the history it would pretend to scrutinize. Within such a 'postmodernist' ideology, a poetics of postmodernism would only self-consciously enact the metalinguistic contradiction of being inside and outside, complicitous and distanced, inscribing and contesting its own provisional formulations. Such an enterprise would obviously not yield any universal truths, but then that would not be what it sought to do. To move from the desire and expectation of sure and single meaning to a recognition of the value of differences and even contradictions might be a tentative first step towards accepting responsibility for both art and theory *as signifying processes*. In other words, maybe we could begin to study the implications of both our *making* and our *making sense* of our culture.

McMaster University, Ontario

REFERENCES

Ackroyd, Peter (1985) *Hawksmoor*. London: Hamish Hamilton.

Banville, John (1976) *Doctor Copernicus*. New York: Norton.

Banville, John (1981) *Kepler*. London: Secker & Warburg.

Barnes, Julian (1984) *Flaubert's Parrot*. London: Cape.

Barth, John (1980) 'The literature of replenishment: postmodern fiction', *The Atlantic* (January), 65–71.

Barthes, Roland (1973) *Mythologies*. Trans. Annette Lavers. London: Granada.

Barthes, Roland (1977) *Image–Music–Text*. Trans. Stephen Heath. New York: Hill & Wang.

Berger, John (1972) *G*. New York: Pantheon.

Berger, Thomas (1964) *Little Big Man*. New York: Dial.

Bertens, Hans (1986) 'The postmodern *Weltanschauung* and its relation with modernism: an introductory survey'. In Fokkema and Bertens 1986, 9–51.

Brooke-Rose, Christine (1981) *A Rhetoric of the Unreal: Studies in Narrative and Structure, Especially of the Fantastic*. Cambridge: Cambridge University Press.

Butler, Christopher (1980) *After the Wake: An Essay on the Contemporary Avant-Garde*. Oxford: Oxford University Press.

Calinescu, Matei (1977) *Faces of Modernity*. Bloomington: Indiana University Press.

Calinescu, Matei (1986) 'Postmodernism and some paradoxes of periodization'. In Fokkema and Bertens 1986, 239–54.

Canary, Robert H. and Kozicki, Henry (eds) (1978) *The Writing of History: Literary Form and Historical Understanding*. Madison: University of Wisconsin Press.

Carmello, Charles (1983) *Silverless Mirrors: Book, Self and Postmodern American Fiction*. Tallahassee: University Presses of Florida.

Carroll, David (1982) *The Subject in Question: The Languages of Theory and the Strategies of Fiction*. Chicago: University of Chicago Press.

Coover, Robert (1977) *The Public Burning*. New York: Viking.

Cortázar, Julio (1978) *A Manual for Manuel*. Trans. Gregory Rabassa. New York: Pantheon.

Crimp, Douglas (1983) 'On the museum's ruins'. In Foster 1983, 43–56.

Culler, Jonathan (1982) *On Deconstruction: Theory and Criticism after Structuralism*. Ithaca, NY: Cornell University Press.

Culler, Jonathan (1983–4) 'At the boundaries: Barthes and Derrida'. In Sussman 1983–4, 23–41.

Cunliffe, Marcus (ed.) (1975) *American Literature Since 1900*. London: Barrie & Jenkins.

Davis, Douglas (1977) *Artculture: Essays on the Post-Modern*. New York: Harper & Row.

de Lauretis, Teresa (1984) *Alice Doesn't: Feminism, Semiotics, Cinema*. Bloomington: Indiana University Press.

Derrida, Jacques (1981) *Positions*. Trans. Alan Bass. Chicago: University of Chicago Press.

D'haen, Theo (1986) 'Postmodernism in American fiction and art'. In Fokkema and Bertens 1986, 211–31.

Doctorow, E.L. (1960) *Welcome to Hard Times*. New York: Simon & Schuster.

Doctorow, E.L. (1971) *The Book of Daniel*. New York: Bantam.

Doctorow, E.L. (1975) *Ragtime*. New York: Random House.

Eagleton, Terry (1985) 'Capitalism, modernism and postmodernism', *New Left Review*, 152, 60–73.

Eco, Umberto (1983) *The Name of the Rose*. Trans. William Weaver. New York: Harcourt, Brace, Jovanovich.

Egbert, Donald D. (1970) *Social Radicalism in the Arts*. New York: Knopf.

Fiedler, Leslie (1975) 'Cross the border – close that gap: postmodernism'. In Cunliffe 1975, 344–66.

Findley, Timothy (1981) *Famous Last Words*. Toronto and Vancouver: Clarke, Irwin.

Fish, Stanley (1986) 'Critical self-consciousness or can we know what we are doing?' Lecture at McMaster University, 4 April 1986.

Fokkema, Douwe (1986) 'Preliminary remarks'. In Fokkema and Bertens 1986, 1–8.

Fokkema, Douwe and Bertens, Hans (eds) (1986) *Approaching Postmodernism*. Amsterdam and Philadelphia: John Benjamins.

Foster, Hal (ed.) (1983) *The Anti-Aesthetic: Essays on Postmodern Culture*. Port Townsend, Washington: Bay Press.

Foucault, Michel (1970) *The Order of Things: An Archaeology of the Human Sciences*. New York: Pantheon.

Foucault, Michel (1972) *The Archaeology of Knowledge and the Discourse on Language*. Trans. A. M. Sheridan Smith. New York: Pantheon.

Fowles, John (1969) *The French Lieutenant's Woman*. Boston and Toronto: Little, Brown.

Fowles, John (1985) *A Maggot*. Toronto: Collins.

Fuentes, Carlos (1964) *The Death of Artemio Cruz*. Trans. Sam Hileman. New York: Farrar, Straus & Giroux.

García Márquez, Gabriel (1971) *One Hundred Years of Solitude*. Trans. Gregory Rabassa. New York: Avon.

Garvin, Harry R. (ed.) (1980) *Romanticism, Modernism, Postmodernism*. Lewisberg: Bucknell University Press. London: Associated University Press.

Ghose, Zulfikar (1983) *The Fiction of Reality*. London: Macmillan.

Giddens, Anthony (1981) 'Modernism and post-modernism', *New German Critique*, 22 (Winter), 15–18.

Gossman, Lionel (1978) 'History and literature: reproduction or signification'. In Canary and Kosicki 1978, 3–39.

Graff, Gerald (1979) *Literature Against Itself*. Chicago: University of Chicago Press.

Graham, Joseph F. (1982) 'Critical persuasion: in response to Stanley Fish'. In Spanos, Bové and O'Hara 1982, 147–58.

Habermas, Jürgen (1983) 'Modernity – an incomplete project'. Trans. Seyla Ben-Habib. In Foster 1983, 3–15.

Harrison, Bernard (1985) 'Deconstructing Derrida'. *Comparative Criticism*, 7, 3–24.

Hassan, Ihab (ed.) (1971) *Liberations: New Essays on the Humanities in Revolution*. Middletown, Conn.: Wesleyan University Press.

Hassan, Ihab (1975) *Paracriticisms: Seven Speculations of the Times*. Urbana: University of Illinois Press.

Hassan, Ihab (1980a) *The Right Promethean Fire: Imagination, Science, and Cultural Change*. Urbana: University of Illinois Press.

Hassan, Ihab (1980b) 'The question of postmodernism'. In Garvin 1980, 117–26.

Hassan, Ihab (1983) 'Postmodernism: a vanishing horizon'. In MLA session, 'Toward a postmodern theory of genre: the new new novel'.

Hassan, Ihab (1986) 'Pluralism in postmodern perspective', *Critical Inquiry*, 12, 3, 503–20.

Hohendahl, Peter Uwe (1982) *The Institution of Criticism*. Ithaca, NY: Cornell University Press.

Hutcheon, Linda (1985) *A Theory of Parody: The Teachings of Twentieth-Century Art Forms*. London and New York: Methuen.

Huyssen, Andreas (1981) 'The search for tradition: avant-garde and postmodernism in the 1970s', *New German Critique*, 22 (Winter), 23–40.

Jameson, Fredric (1983) 'Postmodernism and consumer society'. In Foster 1983, 111–25.

Jameson, Fredric (1984a) 'Postmodernism, or the cultural logic of late capitalism', *New Left Review*, 146 (July–August), 53–92.

Jameson, Fredric (1984b) 'Foreword' to Lyotard 1984a, vii–xxi.

Jencks, Charles (1977) *The Language of Post-Modern Architecture*. London: Academy.

Jencks, Charles (1980a) *Post-Modern Classicism: The New Synthesis*. London: Academy.

Jencks, Charles (1980b) *Late-Modern Architecture and Other Essays*. London: Academy.

Jones, Gayl (1975) *Corregidora*. New York: Random House.

Kamuf, Peggy (1982) 'Replacing feminist criticism', *Diacritics*, 12, 42–7.

Kennedy, William (1978) *Legs*. Harmondsworth: Penguin.

Kingston, Maxine Hong (1981) *China Men*. New York: Ballantine.

Kosinski, Jerzy (1977) *Blind Date*. Boston, Mass.: Houghton Mifflin.

Kosinski, Jerzy (1986) 'Death in Cannes', *Esquire* (March), 81–9.

Kristeva, Julia (1980) 'Postmodernism?' In Garvin 1980, 136–41.

LaCapra, Dominick (1985) *History and Criticism*. Ithaca, NY: Cornell University Press.

Lacoue-Labarthe, Philippe (1984) 'Talks', trans. Christopher Fynsk, *Diacritics*, 14, 3, 24–37.

Lefebvre, Henri (1968) *La Vie quotidienne dans le monde moderne*. Paris: Gallimard.

Lethen, Helmut (1986) 'Modernism cut in half: the exclusion of the avant-garde and the debate on postmodernism'. In Fokkema and Bertens 1986, 233–8.

Lodge, David (1977) *The Modes of Modern Writing: Metaphor, Metonymy, and the Typology of Modern Literature*. London: Edward Arnold.

Lyotard, Jean-François (1983) *Le Différend*. Paris: Minuit.

Lyotard, Jean-François (1984a) *The Postmodern Condition: A Report on Knowledge*. Trans. Geoff Bennington and Brian Massumi. Minneapolis: University of Minnesota Press.

Lyotard, Jean-François (1984b) 'Answering the question: what is postmodernism?' Trans. Régis Durand. In Lyotard 1984a, 71–82.

McCaffery, Larry (1982) *The Metafictional Muse*. Pittsburg: University of Pittsburg Press.

Malmgren, Carl Darryl (1985) *Fictional Space in the Modernist and Postmodernist American Novel*. Lewisburg: Bucknell University Press.

Monod, Jacques (1971) *Chance and Necessity*. New York: Knopf.

Moreno, César Fernández (ed.) (1974) *America Latina en su literatura*. 2nd edn. Buenos Aires: Siglo XXI.

Munro, Alice (1972) *Lives of Girls and Women: A Novel*. New York: McGraw-Hill.

Newman, Charles (1985) *The Post-Modern Aura: The Act of Fiction in an Age of Inflation*. Evanston, Ill.: Northwestern University Press.

Norris, Christopher (1985) *The Contest of Faculties: Philosophy and Theory after Deconstruction*. London and New York: Methuen.

Oliva, Achille Bonito (1984) 'La trans-avanguardia', *Il Verri*, 1–2, 7th series (Marzo–Giugno), 56–79.

Ondaatje, Michael (1976) *Coming Through Slaughter*. Toronto: House of Anansi.

Owens, Craig (1980) 'The allegorical impulse: toward a theory of postmodernism', pt 2, *October*, 13, 59–80.

Palmer, Richard E. (1977) 'Postmodernity and hermeneutics', *Boundary*, 2, 5, 2, 363–93.

Peckham, Morse (1965) *Man's Rage for Chaos: Biology, Behavior, and the Arts*. Philadelphia: Chilton Books.

Portoghesi, Paolo (1983) *Postmodern: The Architecture of the Postindustrial Society*. New York: Rizzoli.

Puig, Manuel (1978–9) *Kiss of the Spider Woman*. New York: Random House.

Pynchon, Thomas (1973) *Gravity's Rainbow*. New York: Viking.

Radhakrishnan, Rajagoplan (1983) 'The post-modern event and the end of logocentrism', *Boundary*, 2, 12, 1, 33–60.

Reed, Ishmael (1972) *Mumbo Jumbo*. Garden City, NY: Doubleday.

Rorty, Richard (1984) 'Deconstruction and circumvention', *Critical Inquiry*, 11, 1, 1–23.

Rushdie, Salman (1982) *Midnight's Children*. London: Picador.

Rushdie, Salman (1983) *Shame*. London: Picador.

Russell, Charles (1980) 'The context of the concept'. In Garvin 1980, 181–93.

Russell, Charles (1985) *Poets, Prophets, and Revolutionaries: The Literary Avant-garde from Rimbaud through Postmodernism*. New York and Oxford: Oxford University Press.

Said, Edward W. (1983) *The World, the Text, and the Critic*. Cambridge, Mass.: Harvard University Press.

Sarduy, Severo (1974) 'El barroco y el neobarroco'. In Moreno 1974, 167–84.

Scott, Chris (1982) *Antichthon*. Montreal: Quadrant.

Sontag, Susan (1967) *Against Interpretation and Other Essays*. New York: Dell.

Spanos, William V., Bové, Paul A. and O'Hara, Daniel (eds) (1982) *The Question of Textuality: Strategies of Reading in Contemporary American Criticism*. Bloomington: Indiana University Press.

Stern, Daniel (1971) 'The mysterious new novel'. In Hassan 1971, 22–37.

Suleiman, Susan Rubin (1986) 'Naming and difference: reflections on "modernism *versus* postmodernism" in literature'. In Fokkema and Bertens 1986, 255–70.

Sussman, Herbert L. (ed.) (1983–4) *At the Boundaries*. Boston, Mass.: Northeastern University Press.

Swan, Susan (1983) *The Biggest Modern Woman of the World*. Toronto: Lester and Orpen Dennys.

Swift, Graham (1983) *Waterland*. London: Heinemann.

Thiher, Allen (1984) *Words in Reflection: Modern Language Theory and Postmodern Fiction*. Chicago: University of Chicago Press.

Thomas, D. M. (1981) *The White Hotel*. Harmondsworth: Penguin.

Todorov, Tzvetan (1981) *Introduction to Poetics*. Trans. Richard Howard. Minneapolis: University of Minnesota Press.

Toulmin, Stephen (1972) *Human Understanding*. 2 vols. Princeton, NJ: Princeton University Press.

Wasson, Richard (1974) 'From priest to Prometheus: culture and criticism in the postmodern period', *Journal of Modern Literature*, 3, 5, 1188–1202.

Watkins, Evan (1978) *The Critical Act: Criticism and Community*. New Haven, Conn., and London: Yale University Press.

Watson, Ian (1975) *The Embedding*. London: Quartet.

Watson, Ian (1983) *Chekhov's Journey*. London: Gollancz.

White, Hayden (1973) *Metahistory: The Historical Imagination in Nineteenth-Century Europe*. Baltimore: Johns Hopkins University Press.

White, Hayden (1978) *Tropics of Discourse: Essays in Cultural Criticism*. Baltimore and London: Johns Hopkins University Press.

White, Hayden (1980) 'The value of narrativity in the representation of reality', *Critical Inquiry*, 7, 1, 5–27.

White, Hayden (1981) 'The narrativization of real events', *Critical Inquiry*, 7, 4, 793–8.

White, Hayden (1984) 'The question of narrative in contemporary historical theory', *History and Theory*, 23, 1–33.

Wiebe, Rudy (1973) *The Temptations of Big Bear*. Toronto: McClelland & Stewart.

Wiebe, Rudy (1977) *The Scorched-Wood People*. Toronto: McClelland & Stewart.

Wilde, Alan (1981) *Horizons of Assent: Modernism, Postmodernism, and the Ironic Imagination*. Baltimore: Johns Hopkins University Press.

Williams, Raymond (1960) *Culture and Society 1780–1950*. Garden City, NY: Doubleday.

Ziolkowski, Theodore (1969) 'Toward a post-modern aesthetics?', *Mosaic*, 2, 4, 112–19.

SIMON DURING

Postmodernism or post-colonialism today

Construction of the concept 'postmodernity' proceeds today at a rapid pace. A welter of articles and books define, elaborate, celebrate and denounce this thing, the postmodern, whose very existence is matter for separate, energetic debate. Clearly interests are at stake, careers are being made. But this activity is finally produced by the concept itself, which, being based on paradox, generates discussion. On the one hand, 'postmodernity' names the loss of critical distance in the world today, and on the other, it names the delegitimation of those categories by which a cultural centre or a socio-economic base might be identified. So writing about postmodernity implies its absence. If there is no critical distance under postmodernity, then how can there be distance enough for analysis of it to proceed? And if it is knowable only as decentred then how can its essence be recognized at all? To be dispersed in this sense is no longer to take the form of an identifiable object. Such paradoxes, which resist closure, produce the deeply problematic object of their attention.

The most persuasive accounts of the postmodern are those – like Jameson's essay 'Postmodernism, or the cultural logic of late capitalism'[1] and like Lyotard's recent work – which remain sensitive to these paralogisms. It is for this reason that I shall be concerned with Jameson and Lyotard here. But, partly in order to escape capture by the paradoxes of postmodernity, my argument will proceed from three positions which counter the conceptual underpinnings of 'postmodernity'.

First, I propose, against Jameson, that postmodernity ought not to be conceived of as 'a cultural dominant'.[2] Next, I want to urge that it is just as rewarding to construe literary postmodernism as an enemy of postmodernity as to consider it as its expression and helpmeet. Thus in ethico-political terms postmodernist texts do not differ from modernist texts which are simultaneously enemies of, and moments in, modernity. (This is to take a different line from that of either liberals like Trilling or Western Marxists like the later Adorno, who see contemporary culture as characterized by the disappearance of adversarial possibilities.) And, third, I take the position that, if there is something that may be called postmodern thought, it too works in ways that cannot be regarded as a mere expression of an underlying postmodernity.

We can, rather brutally, characterize postmodern thought (the phrase is useful rather than happy) as that thought which refuses to turn the Other into the Same. Thus it provides a theoretical space for what postmodernity denies: otherness. Postmodern thought also recognizes, however, that the Other can never speak for itself *as* the Other. One should hesitate to call a discourse which revolves around these positions either for or against post-modernity, but it is certainly not simply consonant with it.

These propositions, none of which is either original or uncontentious, and all of which will be fleshed out below, allow me to mount my central thesis. This is that the concept postmodernity has been constructed in terms which more or less intentionally wipe out the possibility of post-colonial identity. Indeed, intention aside, the conceptual annihilation of the post-colonial condition is actually necessary to any argument which attempts to show that 'we' now live in postmodernity. For me, perhaps eccentrically, post-colonialism is regarded as the need, in nations or groups which have been victims of imperialism, to achieve an identity uncontaminated by universalist or Eurocentric concepts and images. Here the argument becomes complex, since post-colonialism constitutes one of those Others which might derive hope and legitimation from the first aspect of postmodern thought, its refusal to turn the Other into the Same. As such it is threatened by the second moment in postmodern thought.

If postmodernity is regarded as a condition which is dominant today, then the question immediately arises: what else is there? Jameson, for instance, does not cope with this question easily. He conceives of post-modernity as the culture produced by multinational capitalism: a totality which is the effect of another totality. All the cultural phenomena that Jameson refers to instantiate postmodernity. (In fact, he comes ultimately to think of it as so powerful as to be literally inconceivable, that is, as only to be thought of indirectly, as the sublime.) The only tool for analysing an emergence as immense and total as postmodernity is expressive causality. For a theorist as sophisticated as Jameson elsewhere shows himself to be, this represents a retrogressive, not to say a defeatist move.

Jameson inherits these problems. His Hegelian heritage enables him to think both of culture as a totality and of history as a succession of epochs. Indeed, current Marxist accounts of 'postmodernity' are articulated in terms that repeat earlier accounts of modern culture by the Hegelian Marxism of the Frankfurt school. In particular, Adorno's important late essay 'Cultural criticism and society' lies behind Jameson's text. Adorno came to see what he too called late capitalism as a condition in which the world is totally mediated by consciousness. In it, ideology is no longer false consciousness, and high culture becomes 'neutralized'.[3] Adorno also argues that the conceptual underpinning of both transcendental critique (critique from a position outside the phenomena under analysis) and immanent critique (critique from contradictions noted within) has dis-appeared as society has become reified. But Adorno goes further than Jameson. He argues that the Marxist transformation of truth as correspondence into truth as praxis has been absorbed by capitalism as the hegemonic forces have turned pragmatic views of truth to their own ends. And, on the other hand, the counter-attempt to protect areas of culture from instrumental reason now fails because ideology itself has no instrumental function. It has dissolved into distraction, pleasure. Thus the world is now an 'open-air prison'; a place where, in the words of a 1937 essay by Marcuse, which feeds into Adorno's, 'men can feel themselves happy without being so at all.'[4]

Jameson's cultural pessimism, then, is already laid out by Adorno. However, Adorno refers not to postmodernity but to a formation that includes totalitarian and fascist culture. For instance, it is the totalitarian state which has aestheticized existence to the degree that poetry cannot be written after Auschwitz. That famous line does not mean, as is generally supposed, that Auschwitz is too terrible an experience to be written about; it means that writing under fascism and late capitalism has become too trivial to express real horror. The discourse in which Jameson constructs postmodernity was once used, in part, to denounce fascism. (Marcuse's essay would be another point of departure.) This matters, not because analysis of fascism is irrelevant to our culture, but because it allows us to wonder whether the categories of totality and dominance need to be rethought when we turn them to our own times.

Adorno also differs from Jameson when he imagines lines of flight from late capitalism. Jameson sees escape in a postmodern politics whose vocation would be to map the contemporary condition, which he believes to be, under current categories, unmappable. Clearly his own essay believes itself to be engaging in such a politics. Adorno sees escape in a kind of thought 'which strives solely to help the things themselves to that articulation from which they are otherwise cut off by prevailing language'.[5] In almost a liberal spirit, Adorno wishes to provide room for self-determination. True, he cannot offer self-articulation a programme, though the fierce insistence of 'no poetry after Auschwitz' does, rhetorically, free a space in the unfreedom which is our freedom. Jameson's weak call for new forms of mapping, with its emphasis on cognitive knowledge, just like his return to expressive causality, shows how trapped he is compared to Adorno. Perhaps this is so *because* Adorno has a stronger grasp of the contemporary disintegration of cognition, expression and reflection. For he calls not just for knowledge but for action.

Yet – and here we approach the crux of the matter – the weakest moment in Jameson's essay comes when, despite everything, he tries to think postmodernity dialectically. He asks himself how a positive view of its emergence can be taken, and how it permits the forward march of history. He turns to the 'internationalism' of postmodernity. Its progressive task is to realize the end of nationalism so desired by some socialisms. He adds: 'the disastrous realignment of socialist revolution with the older nationalisms (not only in South East Asia), whose results have necessarily aroused such serious recent left reflection, can be adduced in support of this position.'[6] The strongest enemies of postmodernity appear at this weak point: the new post-colonial nationalisms. Indeed, one can be forgiven for thinking that Jameson is harnessing all the power inherent in images of totalitarianism to eradicate cultural difference in the old spirit of enlightened modernity. The reason why one cannot view postmodernity dialectically becomes apparent. As soon as one allows the notion of the 'positive' or 'progressive' to reappear in analysis, the object one has in view is not postmodernity but a stage on the historical journey to the light. And progress, as ever, must be defined by determinate negation – as not the retrogressive, not the residual, not the primitive, not the irrationalism of other cultures. One can say in general, then, that in order to name postmodernity as a cultural dominant expressing itself in postmodern artefacts Jameson has to assume the coming to power of neo-imperialism, and to inflect postmodernity positively he has, for a moment, to become complicit with it.[7]

How to think postmodernity otherwise? How not to read it as the sublime, a totality so powerful as to resist our older knowledge? It seems to me that one must proceed at once on two registers: one archaeological, the other genealogical. (These words are used here at some distance from Foucault.) Postmodernity must be seen as an effect of discrete cultural systems and not as a spirit or epoch, the advance guard of history. The features of postmodernity, which no one has described better than Jameson, are produced within a finite field of what might be called cultural machines: those texts, images, discourses, each formed within particular technologies or media, each with its own way of organizing the intervention on the real, and each with its mode of subject formation.

But postmodernity is known as postmodernity within a discourse which, as we have begun to see, has its own past. Thus to think postmodernity outside the totalizing categories of Western Marxism is to interpret the ideological effects of discrete cultural systems without assuming that these effects take the form of a whole. It is also to reflect on the sources and history of the concepts one uses to describe such effects. There is always a liberating moment when one examines the genealogy of one's discourse. That discourse becomes itself not natural and inevitable but historical, provisional and open to change. In addition to these dual projects of archaeology and genealogy one must also think postmodernity diacritically. Given that 'post-' which rules its usage, it remains a notion which needs to be defined against modernity.

I cannot offer a full reading of what I have called a cultural system here, but let me show what I mean by looking briefly at Coppola's film *Apocalypse Now*. It is an especially good example because it reworks Conrad's modernist classic *Heart of Darkness*, and so allows an entry for diacritical analysis. In turn, *Heart of Darkness* is canonical just because it offers a critique of modernity by breaking down the terms in which European thought distinguished itself from the primitive. Thus if one supposes that postmodernity differs from modernity in the way it legitimates or delegitimates imperialism, or, more radically, if one suspects that the discourse of postmodernity is once again grounded on a denial of otherness, then one would expect *Apocalypse Now* to bear these hypotheses out.

Heart of Darkness shows that the otherness of the primitive is precisely 'our' otherness – where that 'our' indicates, however tentatively, a civilized Eurocentric community. As the title suggests, it is a direct inversion of Enlightenment universalism, which assumes all human beings to be equal in so far as they are led by the light of reason and no further. The valorization of Western reason and civilization becomes for Conrad a cloak for greed, destruction and, paradoxically, the return of irrationality because it allows men to suppose themselves gods. The story makes its point, however, in terms of an old mythic narrative: the voyage to the underground and back, with its known stages and climax. There is therefore a confidence that the culture can narrativize its reneging on enlightenment. The text also has its own positive ideological project. Marlow's voice grafts the discourse of 'the common man' on to that of the sensitive, alienated intellectual. In this way, negative universalism still works towards a consensus. Marlow also attempts, though vainly, to autonomize instrumental reason – vainly, because his work finally fulfils imperialist ends. Finally, the text presents one place in society that is protected from its own truths. Marlow, who knows that enlightenment is a form of barbarism, that the West's Other is the West itself, protects Western women from that truth by lying to them. 'The horror, the horror', Kurtz's last words, are never reported to his fiancée. She continues to believe that he dies with her name on his lips. But there is a twist here. Her values that require protection from the truth *are* the horror too, making Marlow's lie a truth.

Given this summary reading of Conrad's story, one could simply go on to read the film to mark the division between the modern and the post-modern. But the primary shift is one of media and technology, not of meaning. Conrad's tale is *written*: how to catch the voice in writing and which voice to catch are questions it is overtly anxious about. *Apocalypse Now* consists of sounds and images. (This obvious point has a somewhat less obvious corollary. The privileging of the play in writing in current thought is in itself an act of resistance to postmodern technology.) Furthermore, Conrad's novel is the product of a man writing alone at home, autonomously; it requires no investment, no collective enterprise, and thus no high circulation. Although it was written for *Blackwood's Magazine* – no journal being less a vehicle for élitist modernism – the sense that it has no real audience is constantly foregrounded in the story. It is as if the text's implied reader belongs to Kurtz's fiancée's social space, where the truth may not be borne. But Coppola's film, which requires an audience for material reasons, cannot draw any bounds to its audience at all; its implied reader is the abstract consumer, anyone at all.

Because the film is a product of advanced technology, it has quite a different place in the world from that of the novella. In particular, it dissolves the division between truth and lie from quite another direction. Take the scene where Willard – the Marlow figure – first encounters the air cavalry. He jumps out of a helicopter into a blur of violence, noise and danger, in a scene whose production values are so strong that the film seems less the representation of a representation of battle than a recording of actual fighting itself. Suddenly a voice shouts: 'Look like you're fighting!' This is not the entry of postmodern self-referentiality. We soon realize that what we are seeing is, in part, the representation of a representation of a representation: the troops are fighting on and for the television cameras which are gradually panned into sight. Is all this totally fake, then – a mock battle for the folks back home watching the news? No: neither fake nor genuine, or fake *and* genuine. 'Real' bodies litter the ground. The fusion of theatre and war, war as theatre, is a product of modern communications technology and quite foreign to Conrad's moral sense that a lie may tell the truth.

In fact, not only is war theatre, but film is war. If we read (as good consumers) Eleanor Coppola's bestselling account of life on location, we realize that these stunningly realistic battle scenes were made possible by Coppola's hiring arms and equipment from the Filipino army.[8] During shooting these were periodically borrowed back by the army to fight real insurgents in the mountains. And the film set itself was under guard because of fears that it would be attacked for its supplies. The film is enabled by acts of neo-imperialist war: it cannot disengage itself from what it represents. The collapse of distinctions here between making films and making war is not primarily a cultural fact or a theme, but an outcome of specific material conditions. Its effects remain ideological, however: this particular system induces theories of the loss of distance between the image and the imaged.

The derealizing of the world is also an implicit theme of the film. Willard's eyes are constantly shown registering disbelief that the events he witnesses make up reality. But the naïve response to this – 'Better than Disneyland', as one of the soldiers puts it – is inadequate. What the film makes clear is that Vietnam is 'irreal' because principles of intelligibility by which to experience it are missing. In Conrad these principles were narrativity on the one hand, and the unity of the subjective consciousness on the other. Marlow's story and the unity of his response make experiences of imperialist Africa, which he also knows to be unreal and unbelievable, ultimately meaningful. These categories do not work in the film, partly for technical reasons. Shots of Willard's eyes have to do much of the work of presenting subjective response. Yet they can never of themselves show how he interprets what he sees. Even sequences which move metonymically from an expression of disbelief to scenes of horror can only foreground the gap between each shot. The interaction between subjective consciousness and the outer world fails when subjects become visual objects: eyes, mouths, bodies. One might argue that the voice-over could do the work instead, bringing the events into the unity of a sovereign subject's response to them. The disjunction between image and sound in the film prevents that. Willard's voice-over, unlike Marlow's, is not in itself the means *both* of representing events *and* of interpreting them subjectively. In the film the representing function is given over to the camera, blocking control of representation by subjectivity. Thus the autonomy of the bourgeois subject, which depends not only on a clear division of self and world but on a means by which the self can absorb the world, comes apart in film. Here we encounter a moment in the system whose effect is the post-modern sense of the death of the psychological subject and the end of expression.

The film begins with a Doors song entitled 'The End' on the soundtrack as Willard undergoes a nervous breakdown. This breakdown is expressive, but of nothing. After all, nothing has happened to him as yet. The scene seems to be an initial exorcizing of the possibility of expression: after this his only emotion – if emotion it is – is disbelief. But the first scene works against narrative: at the beginning is the end. At the beginning is a horror signifying nothing – or everything – just as at the end. The grounds for the dismantling of narrative progress can, however, be located more precisely. Conrad's narrative is a journey away from light to darkness and back to light as darkness. It requires a world with a boundary between civilization and savagery, even if those distinctions ultimately vanish. Such a difference exists in the film only as quotation. Willard, like Marlow, travels up a river by boat, but messages to him are always in front of him. Helicopters and jets fly above him towards his destination. The form of his journey is unmotivated; it seems a Conradian echo. Because there is no outside to the technology of war, a teleological narrative exists as no more than nostalgia.

Second, the Conradian climaxes which do occur – Kurtz saying 'The horror, the horror' – do so as citation. Just as technology is there before the individual (even Kurtz's compound has radio), Conrad's text is always there before the film itself. This symmetry is much less than an equivalence, however. Coppola is using Conrad's narrative to tell the truth about Vietnam, but in the attempt we are left with historical incongruity and a mere monumentalization of modernism. Kurtz quotes Eliot; he is reading Frazer and Weston; he delivers a Nietzschean tirade on greatness as the capacity to bear the suffering of others. Though he is described as a genius, all this can never add up to charisma. It is the standard matter of a liberal arts education. His true distinction in the film's own terms is his efficiency, his refusal to play the hypocritical game of army bureaucrats. But in having him killed they do not play their own game either – so there is no final difference here. Ultimately, efficiency rules everywhere. The values of honour, truth and work for work's sake, which Conrad upholds as he reveals their limits, have disappeared along with the autonomous subject and work of art.

Finally, there is the question of cultural reproduction. In Conrad's text the story is told to a shadowy 'us' and not the fiancée. Coppola's Kurtz is obsessed with getting his truth told to his son; he entrusts that task to Willard before committing suicide. He and Willard think his truth is unrepresentable, sublime. 'I worry that you might not understand what I have had to be,' he tells Willard. Yet the impossibility of representing Kurtz is not the sublime impossibility of making the boundless conceivable; it is the trivial impossibility of making the secondhand firsthand. Kurtz's greatness is a requirement of narrative climax and intelligibility; it is not in him. A strange consequence emerges: if there is nothing great to tell, if the categories of intelligibility collapse, then it looks as if the culture might not reproduce itself historically. The age of history may disappear into history. Here we catch sight of the way in which postmodernity consumes history, in the sense of nullifying it. It remains an effect rather than an expression or theme.

Yet the failure to reproduce will not happen in silence. After all, Kurtz is on the screen for us all to see. Conrad believed his message to be so dangerous that it might really not have hearers. Coppola's film, which tells us that it bears an image so dangerous as to resist comprehension, requires that the unreproducible be shown everywhere. The true message is that nothing now is unreproducible; it is just that cultural reproduction has divorced itself from cultural values.

These remarks do not make up a full reading of the film, but they offer enough for us to see that it functions as a system creating *effects* of post-modernity within a quite specific technological, economic and ideological frame, rather than an *instance* of that octopus 'postmodernity' or even 'multinational capitalism'. What seems most deeply entrenched in these effects is the encroachment of Western power and technology upon the Third World. The destruction of narrativity is an effect of that power's being able to reach anywhere. The film itself becomes war within the frame of neo-imperialism.

At this point it is worth recalling a final difference between Conrad and Coppola. The original inhabitants of Africa are represented in Conrad's text. It is true that they are falsely presented as cannibals, but they play a role that allows the West to know itself as Other to itself. The Vietnamese enemy are nowhere in Coppola's movie. The film achieves its sense of total irreality by wiping them out of the screen. If the discourse of post-modernity characterizes the postmodern as that which knows no Other, then in this film that Other is eliminated by fiat. If there were an enemy available for representation, perhaps then there would be narrative rather than just citation. In the failure to concede Third World nationalism a right to existence, what is revealed is that will to totality and failure of imagination we have already found in Jameson. This seems more than coincidence. Is there, after all, a secret key with which to unlock post-modernity? If so, can it be found in those who come not to denounce the postmodern like Jameson, nor in that which produces effects of post-modernity, but in that very postmodern thought which is totality's enemy?

For Lyotard, postmodernity is a condition of knowledge at least as much as an epoch. It is a moment within and behind modernity, conceived of again much in the spirit of Marcuse and Adorno. Instead of proposing a history centred on the development of the capitalist mode of production, he thinks of modernity as a process of social rationalization. In his first account of the topic, *The Postmodern Condition*, this process is conceived of negatively: the modern is marked by the emergence of instrumental reason. In modernity, criteria of what he calls 'performaticity' overcome appeals to tradition or metaphysical truth. What counts is not why an act is done or why a thought is thought, but how efficiently and to what immediate end. Applied science is the home of instrumental reason, which (as research) gradually comes to be the standard against which all knowledge is measured.

This development has discursive consequences: cognitive utterances which can be verified and permit control over nature are privileged over those which cannot. But ultimately science cannot validate itself; only its services to power, its instrumentality, permit it to cast a spell of 'self-legitimacy'. The recognition of the failure of science's claim to self-legitimation spells the end for the grand narratives of human emancipation and philosophical speculation. Their collapse reveals a fragmented set of discursive formations and practices. The postmodern just accepts that science itself must act in terms of prescriptives, and cannot validate itself. It must be tolerant of paralogism, seeking no solace from the fragmentation and incommensurability of discourses. And in *The Postmodern Condition*, though not in Lyotard's later work, narrative knowledge takes the place of science as the preferred order.

Lyotard's most recent book, *Le Différend*, though not directly concerned with postmodernism, examines both the moral consequences and the philosophical grounds of discursive heterogeneity.[9] The paradigm for a *différend* is a case in which two parties in dispute cannot articulate their cause in the same idiom. He distinguishes an injury (*un dommage*) from an injustice (*un tort*). In an injustice, the injury is not judged according to the litigant's own criteria of validity, so that the litigant (who then becomes a victim) is in effect silenced. This juridical paradigm is not limited to the courts. The privileging of descriptive statements over prescriptive ones is a *différend* which occurs within end–means rationality; the West places the colonized peoples in a *différend*; capitalism, with its ties to universality, creates a *différend* for the specific, the unexchangeable, and so on.

For Lyotard, in a Cartesian spirit, what exists beyond doubt is the phrase or phrase event. But each phrase occurs as a *différend*: to link one phrase to another is to commit an injustice to possible genres which the first phrase might obligate. Once the nothingness between phrase events is bridged in the interest of a use, as it must be, a *différend* already exists. Thus Lyotard is able to say, 'politics is a matter of linkage between phrases' and is constituted within the 'civil war of language with itself'.[10] Here the Wittgensteinian sense that the limits of language are the limits of the world grasps hands with Derrida's proposition, in his remarks on Lévi-Strauss, that 'violence is writing'.[11] The groundlessness of language, its edging out on to nothing, its character as mere *event*, the fact that it does not exist as a unity declaring its own linkages to itself, all enable the possibility of disagreement, of cultural difference, of violence, as well as the mirage of self-identity.

Unlike Wittgenstein and Derrida, Lyotard returns from these transcendental claims to history. The result disappoints at least as much as it promises. Because language is not a unity, because it necessarily sets *différends* into play, those meta-genres of discourse which claimed to cover all other genres of discourse (speculation) or which promised an end to injustice (narratives of human emancipation) are ungroundable. Philosophy alone is not responsible for their devalidation, however; they die in history. In modern history it becomes impossible to ignore certain cultural *différends*. These *différends* are recognized in the feelings signalled by the silences around certain proper names: Auschwitz is the example he uses most often. No genre of discourse presents itself which would permit a litigant to appeal for justice against the wrong Auschwitz connotes. This silence spells the end of the *grand récits* of Occidental emancipation and speculation which were the secular cover of Western cultural imperialism. Beyond it, no hope of a bridge between heterogeneous discourses survives. One must accept the *différend*.

From the other side, capitalism itself works to undo the force of the order of discourse. In capitalism, money, rather than language, installs exchangeability as the dominant relation between objects in the world. But money is also stored time and security – one might add, stored pleasure. Thus capitalism disburdens itself from notions such as humanity and progress which underpin high-cultural imperialism. But it also discounts the formations which resist these ideas: in particular, nationalism and philosophic deliberation. Ultimately, for Lyotard, capitalism even implies the end of effective political institutions. The play of exchange, the production of money as security, will delegitimate the discursive presuppositions of institutions too. In fact Lyotard's derationalized capitalism is close to Jameson's multinational capitalism, and, like Jameson, Lyotard sees post-colonial nationalism as not just archaic but dangerous. Post-colonial nationalism articulates itself in the 'narrative-mythic'[12] which constructs an immutable cultural origin; it neutralizes the phrase as event, and it projects a 'home' in which difference is suspended; its greatest modern exemplar is Nazism. Thus it too is countered in those names surrounded by silence, pain and, finally, deliberation. Deliberation as doubt leads back to the phrase event, and, if one is not to conspire in the concealment of a *différend*, one must punctuate the ebb and flow of phrases only by 'Arrive-t-il?'

There is here the hope that the breakdown of legitimations for cultural imperialism will free the world both from the spell of instrumental reason and from the nostalgia for mythic origins. It is as if postmodernity would today be the play of post-colonialisms set free not only from the requirement of universality embedded in emancipation, but also from the hunger for identity implicit in narrative as myth. Lyotard aims to clear a space for maximizing the potential of articulation within all idioms. The problem is not just the universalism of Lyotard's own Cartesian approach. Nothing very much in the book softens the shock of the transition from 'Auschwitz' to 'Arrive-t-il?' This last seems a slight result for the promise implicit in his vision of discursive heterogeneity.

For Lyotard, Auschwitz is not only a name with a halo of silence; it produces a particular emotion, signalling a *différend*. Within what context does the binding of this emotion to the name occur? The events at Auschwitz do not come into the world with feelings attached to them as if by nature. Let us think of another name, one which has as little feeling attached to it as any for Western philosophy: New Zealand. This is the country that the Maoris call Aotearoa. When one recalls this, one recalls the massacres, the deaths by introduced diseases, the destruction of a culture and a society which the name New Zealand silences. It is Lyotard's virtue to recognize that mere cognition of these matters can never be enough. How can we account for the difference between the respective silences around the names New Zealand and Auschwitz? One might say, of course, that Auschwitz happened to *us*, whereas New Zealand did not. That, however, would be to assume that we know who we are extra-discursively – by blood; and it is another of Lyotard's virtues that he does not want to concede that either. One might point to a qualitative difference – but how can we measure the loss of a culture against the loss of lives?

Auschwitz resonates for us, not because we are who we are genetically, but because memories of it are constantly circulated orally and in writing. New Zealand's history, on the other hand, is told within a different rhetoric and is barely circulated even inside the country itself. The emotions attached to Auschwitz are attached to language; they remain analytically inseparable from the discourse that produces them. The difference between affect and language begins only when one asks 'Does one have a right to a feeling?' It seems clear that one has a right to articulate the injuries one feels. It is less clear that one has a right to feel feelings as injuries in the first place. In philosophy this question rarely arises because it is generally assumed that an injury is simply felt as an injury, in a way that a bird is not simply seen as a bird. Lyotard does not address himself to the question of the transmission of either language or emotion. If the phrase event is the beginning and end of deliberation, it does not follow that it comes into the world merely bordered by nothingness. It comes transmitted, always already in the history that it makes possible. If philosophy cannot confront the phrase as transmitted, then again that marks a philosophical limit.

What one misses from Lyotard is any sense that a phrase occurs in, or in the gaps of, a particular language. Indeed, on one breathtaking occasion he declares succinctly: 'all *langue* is translatable'.[13] If he were to accept that the question of what is and what is not translatable across languages is interminably debatable, then he would have to accept once again that the limits of specificity within his own frame are not found in the phrase itself. To observe that phrases happen within a particular language is to note a kind other than the phrase: the language the phrase is in. And for philosophical deliberation to confront a particular language at the point where presuppositions end would also and again be to confront a socio-cultural order inseparable from linguistic diversity. This order cannot be covered by the phrase and its linkages. In its flight from categories of totality, Lyotard's linguistic turn evades the one totality – so-called 'natural' language – which it cannot reduce or ignore *on its own terms*. It is precisely to this totality that post-colonialism today appeals.

The post-colonial desire is the desire of decolonized communities for an identity. It belongs to that programme of self-determination which Adorno, unlike Jameson, could envisage. Obviously it is closely connected to nationalism, for those communities are often, though not always, nations. In both literature and politics the post-colonial drive towards identity centres around language, partly because in postmodernity identity is barely available elsewhere. For the post-colonial to speak or write in the imperial tongues is to call forth a problem of identity, to be thrown into mimicry and ambivalence. The question of language for post-colonialism is political, cultural and literary, not in the transcendental sense that the phrase as *différend* enables politics, but in the material sense that a choice of language is a choice of identity.

The link between post-colonialism and language has a history. In his recent book, *Imagined Communities*, Benedict Anderson has argued that nationalism has always been grounded in Babel. That is to say, nationalism is a product of what he calls 'print-capitalism'. He writes: 'the convergence of capitalism and print technology on the fatal diversity of human languages created the possibility of a new form of imagined community which in its basic morphology set the stage for the modern nation.'[14] One does not have to accept the faculty psychology hidden in the phrase 'imagined community' to take the point. Nationalism emerges when some languages get into print and are transmitted through books, allowing subjects to identify themselves as members of the community of readers implied by these books.

Let us take Anderson's history further. Of all the works that created the new print languages, none had more authority than the sacred books. A whiff of heresy attaches itself to the story at this point. The sacred books, as vehicles of God's word, cannot be translated. No doubt, when God reveals himself in natural language, transposition of a kind has already taken place, but the human language becomes divine through the breath of God's voice, the trace of his hand. To deliver the Bible (or the Koran) to *any* demotic language is not just to allow nationalism to overpower the old church, but for meaning to precede form, for communication to precede revelation – it is to admit, in fact, the arbitrariness of the sign.

Anderson does not make a further argument which seems to me inescapable. Once the sign becomes arbitrary, once divine self-revelation becomes transferable across secular languages, then not only may national identities attach to the print language, but language itself no longer permits of any proper identity. If one language can be translated into another, if there is no such thing as a dead language, what untranslatable residue remains to be the property solely of those who speak it; it's form, which cannot be communicated in – as one says – any other form? Yet an identity granted in terms of the signifier (which I use, as it is often used, as a figure for form as such) is an identity that necessarily cannot be communicated. It would seem to be written into the fate of nationalism as print-capitalism that national identity is conferred in the form of its own death warrant. Indeed, there are moments in our culture where an unquenchable nationalist pathos confronts its own mortality: one thinks of Hölderlin's poetry.

The appeal to what is unexchangeable in language is especially tempting under capitalism, which deals with things and words for their exchange value. In the classic formulations of nationalism – Fichte's *Addresses to the German Nation*, for instance – national identity is based on both language (the home of culture) and soil. When a post-colonial nationalist like the Kenyan novelist Ngugi, living under multinational capitalism, looks at the soil, he sees it as a means of production, and means of production do not articulate identities; indeed, where they can be owned, they are often owned by foreigners. This leaves him language and, within language, culture. (One might note that for decolonized nations the other great ground for nationalist pathos – war – has little place. Most post-colonial nations and tribes have a history of defeat by imperialist powers. Freedom is often the enemy's gift.)

Pre-colonial language shelters all the particularity elided over by colonial stereotyping, by modernist valorization of the primitive and by anthropology. In return, as identical to itself, national language excludes the web of contacts, the play of sameness and difference which weave one society into another. It does so in having the advantage that it is not unique. The number of languages available to be spoken is infinite; the economy of Babel is not restricted. And yet language is not identical to itself, and in translation a residue is always left behind.

Ngugi, who places language at the heart of his post-colonialism, was arrested for co-writing plays in Gikuyu, although no doubt his crime was also to aid Gikuyu's transformation into a print language. It is clear that he is not troubled by the sense that an identity given in print language is given as a death warrant. Thus, when he, or someone like him, enters a novel by a post-colonial writer who is disturbed by such questions, the mode of encounter is predictable. Near the beginning of Salman Rushie's novel *Shame*, the narrator is interrupted by such a speaker, disputing his authority to tell the tale.

Outsider! Trespasser! You have no right to this subject! . . . I know: nobody ever arrested me. Nor are they ever likely to. Poacher! Pirate! We reject your authority. We know you, with your foreign language wrapped around you like a flag: speaking about us in your forked tongue, what can you tell but lies? I reply with more questions: Is history to be considered the property of the participants solely? In what courts are such claims staked, what boundary commissions map out the territories?

Can only the dead speak?[15]

This is a dialogue across the bar which internally divides the post-colonial. The divide separates what one can call the post-colonized from the post-colonizers. The post-colonized identify with the culture destroyed by imperialism and its tongue; the post-colonizers, if they do not identify with imperialism, at least cannot jettison the culture and tongues of the imperialist nations. Of course there is not always a choice here. For many ex-colonies the native tongue is the world tongue – English. This is not just true for Australia and Canada, say, as it was once for the United States. It is also true for West Indians as well as for many Maoris and Aboriginals. Indeed, there exists a largely unrecognized but crucial difference in the various post-colonial nations. A country like Australia has almost no possibility of entry into the post-colonized condition, though its neighbour, New Zealand, where Maoris constitute a large minority, does. New Zealand retains a language, a store of proper names, memories of a pre-colonial culture, which seductively figure identity. I have no doubt that the very name New Zealand, and its *différend*, will pass one day, the nation coming to call itself Aotearoa. What one encounters here is a politics of language which rests not on the power within language, the power of rhetoric, but on the power behind language. From the side of the post-colonizer, a return to difference is projected. But, from the side of post-modernity, English (multinational capitalism's tongue) will museumify those pre-colonial languages which have attached themselves to print and the image so belatedly.

Rushdie's dialogue between the post-colonized and the post-colonizer takes place in a language which is not quite transatlantic English. For instance, the position of the adverb in the phrase 'Is history to be considered the property of the participants solely?' marks a tone at the slightest of removes from that English. But its difference may not be invested with nationalist pathos. It remains too close to what is not different but the norm, the language of world power. The sense that Indian, New Zealand, Australian or Irish English is not as different from transatlantic English as French is from English, let alone as different as Maori or Gikuyu, figures the post-colonizer's emptiness. 'Can only the dead speak?' Rushdie elliptically asks, hinting, among other things, at the powerlessness of the pre-colonial tongues and at the death warrant involved in finding an identity through fallen languages, of which his own has fallen furthest.

Rushdie answers the post-colonized challenge in terms of the *différend*. The narrator enquires: 'In what courts are such claims staked?' Now it is he, whose side is not quite that of the oppressed, who appears as victim. He cannot find a place for justice, nor plainly articulate his case, partly because he speaks neither the language of the international market nor a post-colonized language. What he is charged with is what he inherited. If Rushdie, as a post-colonizer, speaks from a place in contemporary history where a *différend* is dramatically foregrounded, then Lyotard's retreat into transcendental philosophy, his mysticism of selected proper names, his preference for experiment, have a strong competitor. If Jameson cannot fully distance himself from the sublimity and internationalism of what we can call image-capitalism, then that is perhaps because he has not listened carefully enough to those voices which talk of the *différend* on its borders.

To consider the *Apocalypse Now* system alongside *Shame* is chastening. The problem is not one of varieties of postmodernism. Rushdie's work is sometimes called postmodern, but it certainly does not reflect post-modernity. *Shame*'s purpose is to reconnect shame – that epic, indeed pre-capitalist, emotion the Greeks called *aidos* – to the recent history of Pakistan. In redirecting shame, the novel calls upon a violence, both feminine and monstrous, which does not, like that of *Apocalypse Now*, reach a climax from the very beginning. *Shame* imagines an unlocalizable, inexpressive, ethically proper violence we never see in *Apocalypse Now*. Indeed, the novel as a whole works in precisely the opposite direction to Coppola's movie. History is not derealized, affect is not atomized into intensity, narrative triumphs, other cultures are not confined within Occidental myth, nor outside the Western screen. So we can say that, when confronted by his post-colonized accuser, Rushdie is startled into an articulation of the problematic of the *différend*, but, when faced with modern Pakistan, he acts as accuser in turn. Here his novel remains connected to those concepts of justice and reason that totalizing denouncers of our postmodernity assure us are in their safekeeping.

University of Melbourne

NOTES

1 Fredric Jameson, 'Postmodernism, or the cultural logic of late capitalism', *New Left Review*, 146 (July–August 1984), pp. 53–91.
2 Ibid., p. 27.
3 Theodor Adorno, 'Cultural criticism and society', in *Prisms*, trans. Samuel and Shierry Weber (London: Neville Spearman, 1967), p. 34.
4 Herbert Marcuse, 'The affirmative character of culture', in *Negations: Essays in Critical Theory*, trans. Jeremy J. Shapiro (London: Allen Lane, 1968), p. 122.
5 Adorno, op. cit., p. 29.
6 Jameson, op. cit., p. 88.
7 This article was written before Jameson's essay 'On magic realism in film' (*Critical Inquiry*, 12 (Winter 1986), pp. 301–25) appeared. It represents a departure from the 'cultural logic' piece because it does allow that post-colonial films differ from postmodern artefacts in ways that offer promise. But from my point of view the essay remains based on doubtful assumptions, i.e.:

   1 Certain 'First World' films (nostalgia films) still *instantiate* postmodernity.
   2 Post-colonial films are more realist than 'First World' films because they are produced in conditions not totally dominated by late capitalism.

3 Post-colonial films are also postmodern in that they exemplify 'denarrativi-zation' and a 'reduction to the body', both of which 'libidinize' cultural residues.

However suggestive an account which moves from these theses may be, it continues to rely on expressive causality and reflection theory; it still assumes that the 'postmodern' and 'realism' are textual features, not effects, or constituted by discourse on texts; and finally it does not allow for the particular mode of ethico-political debate and intervention which takes place only and precisely in post-colonial nations. There is a danger that the post-colonial here becomes both something like Europe before 1848 for Lukács *and* a site saturated by the progressive materialism of postmodernity, rather than a field of forces which postmodern thought must analyse without idealization or condescension.

8 See Eleanor Coppola, *Notes* (New York: Pocket Books, 1979), p. 9.

9 For what follows, see Jean-François Lyotard, *Le Différend* (Paris: Minuit, 1983).

10 Ibid., p. 204.

11 Jacques Derrida, *Of Grammatology*, trans. Gayatri Chakravorty Spivak (Baltimore, Md, and London: Johns Hopkins University Press, 1976), p. 135.

12 Lyotard, op. cit., p. 219.

13 Ibid., p. 226.

14 Benedict Anderson, *Imagined Communities: Reflections on the Origin and Spread of Nationalism* (London: Verso, 1983), ch. 3, 'The origins of national consciousness', p. 49. For further material on this topic, see John Edwards, *Language, Society and Identity* (Oxford: Basil Blackwell, 1985), 'Language and nationalism'.

15 Salman Rushdie, *Shame* (New York: Vintage Books, 1984), p. 23.

JONATHAN DOLLIMORE

Different desires: subjectivity and transgression in Wilde and Gide

In Blidah, Algeria, in January 1895 André Gide is in the hall of a hotel, about to leave. His glance falls on the slate which announces the names of new guests: 'suddenly my heart gave a leap; the two last names . . . were those of Oscar Wilde and Lord Alfred Douglas.'[1] Acting on his first impulse, Gide 'erases' his own name from the slate and leaves for the station. Twice thereafter Gide writes about the incident, unsure why he left so abruptly; first in his *Oscar Wilde* (1901), then in *Si le grain ne meurt (If It Die*, 1920, 1926). It may, he reflects, have been a feeling of *mauvaise honte* or of embarrassment: Wilde was becoming notorious and his company compromising. But also he was severely depressed, and at such times 'I feel ashamed of myself, disown, repudiate myself'.[2] Whatever the case, on his way to the station he decides that his leaving was cowardly and so returns. The consequent meeting with Wilde was to precipitate a transformation in Gide's life and subsequent writing.

Gide's reluctance to meet Wilde certainly had something to do with previous meetings in Paris four years earlier in 1891; they had seen a great deal of each other across several occasions, and biographers agree that this was one of the most important events in Gide's life. But these meetings had left Gide feeling ambivalent towards the older man, and it is interesting that not only does Gide say nothing in *If It Die* about Wilde's obvious and deep influence upon him in Paris in 1891, but, according to Jean Delay, in the manuscript of Gide's journal the pages corresponding to that period – November–December 1891 – are torn out.[3]

Undoubtedly Gide was deeply disturbed by Wilde, and not surprisingly, since Gide's remarks in his letters of that time suggest that Wilde was intent on undermining the younger man's self-identity, rooted as it was in a Protestant ethic and high bourgeois moral rigour and repression that generated a kind of conformity to which Wilde was, notoriously, opposed. Wilde wanted to encourage Gide to transgress. It may be that he wanted to re-enact in Gide the creative liberation – which included strong criminal identification – which his own exploration of transgressive desire had produced nine years earlier. (Wilde's major writing, including that which constitutes his transgressive aesthetic, dates from 1886 when, according to Robert Ross, he first practised homosexuality.[4]) But first Wilde had to undermine that law-full sense of self which kept Gide transfixed within the law. So Wilde tried to decentre or demoralize Gide – 'demoralize' in the sense of liberate from moral constraint rather than to dispirit; or, rather, to dispirit precisely in the sense of to liberate from a morality anchored in the very notion of spirit. ('Demoralize' was a term Gide remembers Wilde using in just this sense, one which, for Gide, recalled Flaubert.) Hence, perhaps, those most revealing of remarks by Gide to Valéry at this time (4 December 1891):

> Wilde is religiously contriving to kill what remains of my soul, because he says that in order to know an essence, one must eliminate it: he wants me to miss my soul. The measure of a thing is the effort made to destroy it. Each thing is made up only of its emptiness.

And in another letter of the same month: 'Please forgive my silence: since Wilde, I hardly exist anymore.'[5] And in unpublished notes for this time he declares that Wilde was 'always trying to instil into you *a sanction for evil*'.[6] So, despite his intentions to the contrary, Wilde at that time seems indeed to have dispirited Gide in the conventional sense. Yet perhaps the contrary intention was partly successful; on 1 January 1892 Gide writes: 'Wilde, I think, did me nothing but harm. In his company I had lost the habit of thinking. I had more varied emotions, but had forgotten how to bring order into them.'[7] In fact, Gide reacted, says Delay, in accordance with his Protestant instincts, reaffirming a moral conviction inseparable from an essentialist conception of self (cf. *Journal*, 29 December 1891: 'O Lord keep me from evil. May my soul again be proud'). Even so, this meeting with Wilde is to be counted as one of the most important events in Gide's life: 'for the first time he found himself confronted with a man who was able to bring about, within him, a transmutation of all values – in other words, a revolution.'[8] Richard Ellmann concurs with this judgement, and suggests further that Wilde's attempt to 'authorize evil' in Gide supplies much of the subject of *The Immoralist* and *The Counterfeiters*, the former work containing a character, Ménalque, who is based upon Wilde.[9]

It is against the background and the importance of that earlier meeting, together with the ambivalence towards Wilde which it generated in Gide, that we return to that further encounter in Algeria four years later. If anything, the ambivalence seems even stronger; in a letter to his mother Gide describes Wilde as a terrifying man, a 'most dangerous product of modern civilization' who had already depraved Douglas '*right down to the marrow*'.[10] A few days later Gide meets them again in Algiers, a city which Wilde declares his intention to demoralize.[11] It is here that there occurs the event which was to change Gide's life and radically influence his subsequent work, an event for which the entire narrative of *If It Die* seems to have been preparing. He is taken by Wilde to a café. It is there that 'in the half-open doorway, there suddenly appeared a marvellous youth. He stood there for a time, leaning with his raised elbow against the door-jamb, and outlined on the dark background of the night.' The youth joins them; his name is Mohammed; he is a musician; he plays the flute. Listening to that music, 'you forgot the time and place, and who you were'.[12] This is not the first time Gide has experienced this sensation of forgetting. Africa increasingly attracts him in this respect;[13] there he feels liberated and the burden of an oppressive sense of self is dissolved: 'I laid aside anxieties, constraints, solicitudes, and as my will evaporated, I felt myself becoming porous as a beehive.'[14] Now, as they leave the café, Wilde turns to Gide and asks him if he desires the musician. Gide writes: 'how dark the alley was! I thought my heart would fail me; and what a dreadful effort of courage it needed to answer: "yes", and with what a choking voice!' (Delay points out that the word 'courage' is here transvalued by Gide; earlier he had felt courage was needed for self-discipline, whereas now it is the strength to transgress.[15])

Wilde arranges something with their guide, rejoins Gide and then begins laughing: 'a resounding laugh, more of triumph than of pleasure, an interminable, uncontrollable, insolent laugh . . . it was the amusement of a child and a devil'. Gide spends the night with Mohammed: 'my joy was unbounded, and I cannot imagine it greater, even if love had been added.' Though not his first homosexual experience, it confirmed his (homo)sexual 'nature', what, he says, was 'normal' for him. Even more defiantly Gide declares that, although he had achieved 'the summit of pleasure five times' with Mohammed, 'I revived my ecstasy many more times, and back in my hotel room I relived its echoes until morning'[16] (this passage was one of those omitted from some English editions). At this suitably climactic moment we postpone further consideration of Gide and turn to the anti-essentialist, transgressive aesthetic which Wilde was advocating and which played so important a part in Gide's liberation or corruption, depending on one's point of view. And I want to begin with an indispensable dimension of that aesthetic: one for which Wilde is yet hardly remembered – or, for some of his admirers, one which is actively forgotten – namely, his advocacy of socialism.

Wilde begins his *The Soul of Man under Socialism* (1891) by asserting that a socialism based on sympathy alone is useless; what is needed is to '*try and reconstruct society on such a basis that poverty will be impossible*'. It is precisely because Christ made no attempt to reconstruct society that he had to resort to pain and suffering as the exemplary mode of self-realization. The alternative is the socialist commitment to transforming the material conditions which create and perpetuate suffering. One might add that, if the notion of redemption through suffering has been a familiar theme within English studies, this only goes to remind us of the extent to which, in the twentieth century, criticism has worked in effect as a displaced theology or as a vehicle for an acquiescent quasi-religious humanism. So Wilde's terse assertion in 1891 that 'Pain is not the ultimate mode of perfection. It is merely provisional and a protest'[17] may still be an appropriate response to those who fetishize suffering in the name, not of Christ, but of the tragic vision and the human condition (sainthood without God, as Camus once put it).

Wilde also dismisses the related pieties, that humankind learns wisdom through suffering, and that suffering humanizes. On the contrary, 'misery and poverty are so absolutely degrading, and exercise such a paralysing effect over the nature of men, that no class is ever really conscious of its suffering. They have to be told of it by other people, and they often entirely disbelieve them.' Against those who were beginning to talk of the dignity of manual labour, Wilde insists that most of that too is absolutely degrading. Each of these repudiations suggests that Wilde was fully aware of how exploitation is crucially a question of ideological mystification as well as of outright coercion: 'to the thinker, the most tragic fact in the whole of the French Revolution is not that Marie Antoinette was killed for being a queen, but that the starved peasant of the Vendée voluntarily went out to die for the hideous cause of feudalism.' Ideology reaches into experience and identity, re-emerging as 'voluntary' self-oppression. But it is also the ruling ideology which prevents the rulers themselves from seeing that it is not sin that produces crime but starvation, and that the punishment of the criminal escalates rather than diminishes crime and also brutalizes the society which administers it even more than the criminal who receives it.[18]

There is much more in this essay, but I have summarized enough to show that it exemplifies a tough materialism; in modern parlance one might call it anti-humanist, not least because for Wilde a radical socialist programme is inseparable from a critique of those ideologies of subjectivity which seek redemption in and through the individual. A case in point would be Dickens's treatment of Stephen Blackpool in *Hard Times* (Wilde made a point of disliking Dickens); another might be Arnold's assertion in *Culture and Anarchy*: 'Religion says: "*The Kingdom of God is within you*"; and culture, in like manner, places human perfection in an *internal* condition, in the growth and predominance of our humanity proper.'[19] But isn't a category like anti-humanism entirely inappropriate, given Wilde's celebration of individualism? The term itself, anti-humanism, is not worth fighting over; I have introduced it only as a preliminary indication of just how different is Wilde's concept of the individual from that which has prevailed in idealist culture generally and English studies in particular. It is this difference which the next section considers.

INDIVIDUALISM

In Wilde's writing, individualism is less to do with a human essence, Arnold's inner condition, than a dynamic social potential, one which implies a radical possibility of freedom 'latent and potential in mankind generally'. Thus individualism as Wilde conceives it generates a 'disobedience [which] in the eyes of anyone who has read history, is man's original virtue. It is through disobedience that progress has been made, through disobedience and through rebellion.'[20] Under certain conditions there comes to be a close relationship between crime and individualism, the one generating the other.[21] Already, then, Wilde's notion of individualism is inseparable from transgressive desire and a transgressive aesthetic. Hence, of course, his attack on public opinion, mediocrity and conventional morality, all of which forbid both the desire and the aesthetic.[22]

The public which Wilde scorns is that which seeks to police culture; which is against cultural difference; which reacts to the aesthetically unconventional by charging it with being either grossly unintelligible or grossly immoral. Far from reflecting or prescribing for the true nature or essence of man, individualism will generate the cultural difference and diversity which conventional morality, orthodox opinion and essentialist ideology disavow. Wilde affirms the principle of differentiation to which all life grows and insists that selfishness is not living as one wishes to live, but asking others to live as one wishes to live, trying to create 'an absolute uniformity of type'. And unselfishness not only recognizes cultural diversity and difference but enjoys them. Individualism as an affirmation of cultural as well as personal difference is therefore fundamentally opposed to that 'immoral ideal of uniformity of type and conformity to rule which is so prevalent everywhere, and is perhaps most obnoxious in England'.[23]

Uniformity of type and conformity to rule: Wilde despises these imperatives not only in individuals but as attributes of class and ruling ideologies. Wilde's Irish identity is a crucial factor in his oppositional stances, and it is instructive to consider in this connection a piece written two years earlier, in 1889, where he addresses England's exploitation and repression of Ireland. 'Mr Froude's Blue Book' is a review of J. A. Froude's novel, *The Two Chiefs of Dunboy*. In the eighteenth century, says Wilde, England tried to rule Ireland 'with an insolence that was intensified by race-hatred and religious prejudice'; in the nineteenth, with 'a stupidity . . . aggravated by good intentions'. Froude's picture of Ireland belongs to the earlier period, and yet to read Wilde's review now makes one wonder what if anything has changed in Tory 'thinking' except that possibly now the one vision holds for both Ireland and the mainland:

> Resolute government, that shallow shibboleth of those who do not understand how complex a thing the art of government is, is [Froude's] posthumous panacea for past evils. His hero, Colonel Goring, has the words Law and Order ever on his lips, meaning by the one the enforcement of unjust legislation, and implying by the other the suppression of every fine natural aspiration. That the government should enforce iniquity, and the governed submit to it, seems to be to Mr Froude, as it certainly is to many others, the true ideal of political science. . . . Colonel Goring . . . Mr Froude's cure for Ireland . . . is a '*Police* at any price' man.[24]

Individualism joins with socialism to abolish other kinds of conformity, including, says Wilde, family life and marriage, each being unacceptable because rooted in and perpetuating the ideology of property.[25] Individualism is both desire for a radical personal freedom and a desire for society itself to be radically different, the first being inseparable from the second. So Wilde's concept of the individual is crucially different from that sense of the concept which signifies the private, experientially self-sufficient, autonomous, bourgeois subject; indeed, for Wilde, 'Personal experience is a most vicious and limited circle' and 'to know anything about oneself one must know all about others'.[26] Typically, within idealist culture, the experience of an essential subjectivity is inseparable from knowledge of that notorious transhistorical category, human nature. This is Wilde on human nature: 'the only thing that one really knows about human nature is that it changes. Change is the one quality we can predicate of it.'[27] To those who then say that socialism is incompatible with human nature and therefore impractical, Wilde replies by rejecting practicality itself as presupposing and endorsing both the existing social conditions and the concept of human nature as fixed, each of which suppositions socialism would contest: 'it is exactly the existing conditions that one objects to . . . [they] will be done away with, and human nature will change.'[28] Elsewhere Wilde accepts that there is *something* like human nature, but, far from being the source of our most profound being, it is actually ordinary and boring, the least interesting thing about us. It is where we differ from each other that is of definitive value.[29]

ART VERSUS LIFE

The key concepts in Wilde's aesthetic are protean and shifting, not least because they are paradoxically and facetiously deployed. When, for example, he speaks of life – 'poor, probable, uninteresting human life'[30] – or reality as that to which art is opposed, he means different things at different times. One of the most interesting and significant referents of concepts like life and reality, as Wilde uses them, is the prevailing social order. Even nature, conceived as the opposite of culture and art, retains a social dimension,[31] especially when it signifies ideological mystification of the social. That is why Wilde calls being natural a 'pose', and an objectionable one at that, precisely because it seeks to mystify the social as natural.[32]

Nature and reality signify a prevailing order which art ignores and which the critic negates, subverts and transgresses. Thus, for example, the person of culture is concerned to give 'an accurate description of what has never occurred', while the critic sees 'the object as in itself it really is not'[33] (Wilde is here inverting the proposition which opens Arnold's famous essay 'The function of criticism at the present time'). Not surprisingly, then, criticism and art are aligned with individualism against a prevailing social order; a passage which indicates this is also important in indicating the basis of Wilde's aesthetic of transgressive desire: 'Art is Individualism and Individualism is *a disturbing and disintegrating force*. Therein lies its immense value. For what it seeks to disturb is monotony of type, slavery of custom, tyranny of habit.'[34] Art is also self-conscious and critical; in fact, 'self-consciousness and the critical spirit are one'.[35] And art, like individualism, is oriented towards the realm of transgressive desire: 'What is abnormal in Life stands in normal relations to Art. It is the only thing in

Life that stands in normal relations to Art.'[36] One who inhabits that realm, 'the cultured and fascinating liar', is both an object and source of desire.[37] The liar is important because s/he contradicts not just conventional morality but its sustaining origin, 'truth'. So art runs to meet the liar, kissing his 'false beautiful lips, knowing that he alone is in possession of the great secret of all her manifestations, the secret that Truth is entirely and absolutely a matter of style'. Truth, the epistemological legitimation of the real, is rhetorically subordinated to its antitheses – appearance, style, the lie – and thereby simultaneously both appropriated and devalued. Reality, also necessarily devalued and demystified by the loss of truth, must imitate art, while life must meekly follow the liar.[38]

Further, life is at best an energy which can only find expression through the forms that art offers it. But form is another slippery and protean category in Wilde's aesthetic. In one sense Wilde is a proto-structuralist: 'Form is the beginning of things. . . . The Creeds are believed, not because they are rational, but because they are repeated. . . . Form is everything. . . . Do you wish to love? Use Love's Litany, and the words will create the yearning from which the world fancies that they spring.'[39] Here form is virtually synonymous with culture. Moreover, it is a passage in which Wilde recognizes the priority of the social and the cultural in determining meaning, even in determining desire. So for Wilde, although desire is deeply at odds with society in its existing forms, it does not exist as a pre-social authenticity; it is within and in-formed by the very culture which it also transgresses.

TRANSGRESSION AND THE SENSE OF SELF

Returning now to Gide, we are in a position to contrast his essentialism with Wilde's anti-essentialism, a contrast which epitomizes one of the most important differences within the modern history of transgression. In a way that perhaps corresponds to his ambivalence towards Wilde, Gide had both submitted to and resisted the latter's attempts to undermine his sense of self. Both the submission and the resistance are crucial for Gide's subsequent development as a writer and, through Gide's influence, for modern literature. The submission is apparent enough in the confirmation of his homosexual desire and the way this alters his life and work. In 1924 he published *Corydon*, a courageous defence of homosexuality which he later declared to be his most important book (*Journal*, 19 October 1942). In *Corydon* he did not just demand tolerance for homosexuality but also insisted that it was not contrary to nature but intrinsically natural; that heterosexuality prevails merely because of convention; that historically homosexuality is associated with great artistic and intellectual achievement, while heterosexuality is indicative of decadence. About these provocative and suspect claims I have only the space to observe that the fury they generated in the majority of commentators is as significant as Gide's reasons for making them in the first place. Two years later Gide published the equally controversial commercial edition of *If It Die*, which, as already indicated, contained, for that time, astonishingly explicit accounts of his homosexuality, and for which, predictably, Gide was savagely castigated. Much later still, Gide was to write to Ramon Fernandez, confirming that 'sexual non-conformity is the first key to my works'; the experience of his own deviant desire leads him first to attack sexual conformity and then 'all other sphinxes of conformity', suspecting them to be 'the brothers and cousins of the first'.[40]

But Gide – having with Wilde both allowed and encouraged the subversion of an identity which had hitherto successfully, albeit precariously, repressed desire – does not then substitute for it the decentred subjectivity which animates Wilde's aesthetic; on the contrary, he reconstitutes himself as an essentially new self. Michel in *The Immoralist* (1902) corresponds in some measure to Gide in Algiers (while, as earlier remarked, another character in that novel, Ménalque, is probably based on Wilde). For Michel, as for Gide, transgression does not lead to a relinquishing of self but to a totally new sense of self. Michel throws off the culture and learning which up to that point had been his whole life, in order to find himself: that 'authentic creature that had lain hidden beneath . . . whom the Gospel had repudiated, whom everything about me – books, masters, parents, and I myself had begun by attempting to suppress. . . . Thenceforward I despised the secondary creature, the creature who was due to teaching, whom education had painted on the surface.' He composes a new series of lectures in which he shows 'Culture, born of life, as the destroyer of life'. The true value of life is bound up with individual uniqueness: 'the part in each of us that we feel is different from other people is the part that is rare, the part that makes our special value.'[41]

Whereas for Wilde transgressive desire leads to a relinquishing of the essential self, for Gide it leads to a discovery of the authentic self. As he writes in *If It Die*, it was at that time in Algiers that 'I was beginning to discover myself – and in myself the tables of a new law'.[42] And he writes to his mother on 2 February 1895: 'I'm unable to write a line or a sentence so long as I'm not in *complete possession* (that is, WITH FULL KNOWLEDGE) of myself. I should like very submissively to follow nature – the unconscious, which is within myself and must be *true*.'[43] Here again there is the indirect yet passionate insistence on the naturalness, the authenticity of his deviant desire. With that wilful integrity – itself a kind of perversity? – rooted in Protestantism, Gide not only appropriates dominant concepts (the normal, the natural) to legitimate his own deviation, but goes so far as to claim a sanction for deviation in the teachings of Christ.[44] (In his journal for 1893 (detached pages) he wrote: 'Christ's saying is just as true in art: "Whoever will save his life (his personality) shall lose it".' He later declared, after reading Nietzsche's *Thus Spake Zarathustra*, that it was to this that Protestantism led, 'to the greatest liberation'.[45]) Delay contends, plausibly, that some of the great Gidean themes, especially those entailing transgression, can be found in the rebellious letters that he wrote to his mother in March 1895, letters inspired by his self-affirmation as a homosexual.[46]

It would be difficult to overestimate the importance, in the recent history of Western culture, of transgression in the name of an essential self which is the origin and arbiter of the true, the real and the moral – that is, the three main domains of knowledge in Western culture: the epistemological, the ontological and the ethical. Its importance within the domain of sexuality and within discourses which intersect with sexuality is becoming increasingly apparent, but it has been central also in liberation movements which have not primarily been identified with either of these. This, finally, is Gide in 1921:

> The borrowed truths are the ones to which one clings most tenaciously, and all the more so since they remain foreign to our intimate self. It takes much more precaution to deliver one's own message, much more boldness and prudence, than to sign up with and add one's voice to an already existing party. . . . I believed that it is above all to oneself that it is important to remain faithful.[47]

PARADOX AND PERVERSITY

The contrast between Gide and Wilde is striking: not only are Wilde's conceptions of subjectivity and desire anti-essentialist but so too – and consequently – is his advocacy of transgression. Deviant desire reacts against, disrupts and displaces from within; rather than seeking to escape the repressive ordering of sexuality, Wilde reinscribes himself within and relentlessly inverts the binaries upon which that ordering depends. Inversion, rather than Gide's escape into a pre- or trans-social reality, defines Wilde's transgressive aesthetic. In Gide, transgression is in the name of a desire and identity rooted in the natural, the sincere and the authentic; Wilde's transgressive aesthetic is the reverse: *in*sincerity, *in*authenticity and *un*naturalness become the liberating attributes of decentred identity and desire, and inversion becomes central to Wilde's expression of this aesthetic, as can be seen from a selection of his *Phrases and Philosophies for the Use of the Young* (1894):

> If one tells the truth, one is sure, sooner or later, to be found out.
> Only the shallow know themselves.
> To be premature is to be perfect.
> It is only the superficial qualities that last. Man's deeper nature is soon found out.
> To love oneself is the beginning of a lifelong romance.[48]

In Wilde's writings a non-centred or dispersed desire is both the impetus for a subversive inversion *and* what is released by it. Perhaps the most general inversion operating in his work reverses that most dominating of binaries, nature/culture; more specifically, the attributes on the left are substituted for those on the right:

	X	for	Y
	surface		depth
	lying		truth
	change		stasis
	difference		essence
	persona/role		essential self
	abnormal		normal
	insincerity		sincerity
	style/artifice		authenticity
	facetious		serious
	narcissism		maturity

For Michel in *The Immoralist* and to an extent for Gide himself, desire may be proscribed, but this does not affect its authenticity; if anything, it confirms it. In a sense, then, deviant desire is legitimated in terms of culture's opposite, nature, or, in a different but related move, in terms of something which is pre-cultural or *always more than* cultural. Gide shares with the dominant culture an investment in the Y column above; he appropriates its categories *from* the dominant *for* the subordinate. In contrast, for Wilde transgressive desire is both rooted in culture and the impetus for affirming different/alternative kinds of culture. So what in Gide's conception of transgression might seem a limitation or even a confusion – namely, that the desire which culture outlaws is itself thoroughly cultural – in fact facilitates one of the most disturbing of all forms of transgression: the outlaw turns up as inlaw; more specifically, that which society forbids Wilde reinstates through and within some of its most cherished and central cultural categories – art, the aesthetic, art criticism, individualism. At the same time as he appropriates those categories he also transvalues them through inversion, thus making them now signify those binary exclusions (the X column) by which the dominant culture knows itself (thus abnormality is not just the opposite, but *the necessarily always present* antithesis of normality). It is an uncompromising inversion, this being the (perversely) appropriate strategy for a transgressive desire which is of its 'nature', according to this culture, an inversion.

But inversion has a specific as well as a general target: as can be seen from the *Phrases and Philosophies* just quoted, Wilde seeks to subvert those dominant categories which signify *subjective depth*. Such categories (the Y column) are precisely those which ideologically identify (interpellate?) the mature adult individual, which confer or ideologically coerce identity. And they too operate in terms of binary contrast: the individual knows what he – I choose the masculine pronoun deliberately[49] – is in contrast to what he definitely is not or should not be. In Wilde's inversions, the excluded inferior term returns as the *now superior* term of a related series of binaries. Some further examples of Wilde's subversion of subjective depth are:

A little sincerity is a dangerous thing, and a great deal is absolutely fatal.[50]

All bad poetry springs from genuine feeling.[51]

In matters of grave importance, style, not sincerity, is the *vital* thing.[52]

Only shallow people . . . do not judge by appearances.[53]

Insincerity . . . is merely a method by which we can multiply our personalities. Such . . . was Dorian Gray's opinion. He used to wonder at the shallow psychology of those who conceived the Ego in man as a thing simple, permanent, reliable, and of one essence. To him man was a being with myriad lives and myriad sensations, a complex, multiform creature.[54]

At work here is a transgressive desire which makes its opposition felt as a disruptive reaction upon, and inversion of, the categories of subjective depth which hold in place the dominant order which proscribes that desire.

THE DECENTRED SUBJECT AND THE QUESTION OF THE POSTMODERN

Wilde's transgressive aesthetic relates to at least three aspects of contemporary theoretical debates: first, the dispute about whether the inversion of binary opposites subverts or, on the contrary, reinforces the order which those binaries uphold; second, the political importance – or irrelevance – of decentring the subject; third, postmodernism and one of its more controversial criteria: the so-called disappearance of the depth model, especially the model of a deep human subjectivity. Since the three issues closely relate to each other, I shall take them together.

It might be said that Wildean inversion disturbed nothing; by merely reversing the terms of the binary, inversion remains within its limiting framework: the world turned upside down can only be righted, not changed. Moreover, the argument might continue, Wilde's paradoxes are superficial in the pejorative sense of being inconsequential, of making no difference. But we should remember that in the first of the three trials involving Wilde in 1895 he was cross-examined on his *Phrases and Philosophies*, the implication of opposing counsel being that they, along with *Dorian Gray*, were 'calculated to subvert morality and encourage unnatural vice'.[55] There is a sense in which evidence cannot get more material than this, and it remains so whatever our retrospective judgement about the crassness of the thinking behind such a view.

One of the many reasons why people thought as they did was to do with the perceived connections between Wilde's aesthetic transgression and his sexual transgression. It is not only that at this time the word 'inversion' was being used for the first time to define a specific kind of deviant sexuality and deviant person (the two things now being indissociable), but also that, in producing the homosexual as a species of being rather than, as before, seeing sodomy as an aberration of behaviour,[56] society now regarded homosexuality as rooted in a person's identity; this sin might pervade all aspects of an individual's being, and its expression might become correspondingly the more insidious and subversive. Hence in part the animosity and hysteria directed at Wilde during and after his trial.

After he had been found guilty of homosexual offences and sentenced to two years' imprisonment with hard labour, the editorial of the London *Evening News* subjected him to a vicious and revealing homophobic attack. He had, it claimed, tried to subvert the 'wholesome, manly, simple ideals of English life'; moreover, his 'abominable vices . . . were the natural outcome of his diseased intellectual condition'. The editorial also saw Wilde as the leader of a likeminded but younger subculture in London.[57] The view expressed here was, and indeed remains, for some, a commonplace: sexual deviation is symptomatic of a much wider cultural deterioration and/or subversion. There is an important sense in which Wilde confirmed and exploited this connection between discursive and sexual perversion: 'What the paradox was to me in the sphere of thought, perversity became to me in the sphere of passion.'[58] This feared crossover between discursive and sexual perversion has sanctioned terrible brutalities against homosexuals, at the same time, at least in this period, it was also becoming the medium for what Foucault calls a reverse or counter-discourse,[59] giving rise to what is being explored here in relation to Wilde – what might be called the politics of inversion/perversion (again crossing over and between the different senses of these words). Derrida has argued persuasively for binary inversion as a politically indispensable stage towards the eventual displacement of the binary itself.[60] The case of Wilde indicates, I think, that in actual historical instances of inversion – that is, inversion as a strategy of cultural struggle – it already constitutes a displacement, if not of the binary itself, then certainly of the moral and political norms which cluster dependently around its dominant pole.

We begin to see, then, why Wilde was hated with such an intensity, even though he rarely advocated in his published writings any explicitly immoral practice. What held those 'wholesome, manly, simple ideals of English life' in place were traditional and conservative ideas of what constituted human nature and human subjectivity, and it was *these* that Wilde attacked: not so much conventional morality itself as the ideological anchor points for that morality, namely notions of identity as subjective depth, whose criteria appear in the Y column above. And so it might be said that here, generally, as he did with Gide more specifically, Wilde subverts the dominant categories of subjectivity which keep desire in subjection, and subverts the essentialist categories of identity which keep morality in place. Even though there may now be a temptation to patronize and indeed dismiss both the Victorians' 'wholesome, manly, simple ideals of English life' and Wilde's inversion of them, the fact remains that, in successively reconstituted forms, those ideals, *together with* the subject positions which instantiate them, come to form the moral and ethical base of English studies in our own century, and, indeed, remain culturally central today.

I am thinking here not just of the organicist ideology so characteristic of an earlier phase of English studies, one that led, for example, to the celebration of Shakespeare's alleged 'national culture, rooted in the soil and appealing to a multi-class audience', but more specifically and importantly of what Chris Baldick in his excellent study goes on to call its 'subjective correlative', namely, the *'maintenance of the doctrine of psychic wholeness in and through literature as an analogue for a projected harmony and order in society'*.[61] For I. A. Richards, all human problems (continues Baldick) become problems of mental health, with art as the cure, and literary criticism becomes 'a question of attaining the right state of mind to judge other minds, according to their degree of immaturity, inhibition, or perversion'. As Richards himself puts it, sincerity 'is the quality we most insistently require in poetry. It is also the quality we most need as critics.'[62] As a conception of both art and criticism, this is the reverse of Wilde's. Similarly with the Leavises, whose imperative concept was the related one of 'maturity', one unhappy consequence of which was their promotion of the 'fecund' D. H. Lawrence against the perverse W. H. Auden. As Baldick goes on to observe, 'this line of critics is not only judicial in tone but positively inquisitorial, indulging in a kind of perversion-hunting' which is itself rooted in 'a simple model of [pre- or anti-Freudian] normality and mental consistency'.[63]

This tradition has, of course, been subjected to devastating critiques in recent years; in particular, its notions of subjective integration and psychic wholeness have been attacked by virtually all the major movements within contemporary critical theory including Marxism, structuralism, post-structuralism and psychoanalysis. Yet Wilde's subversion of these notions is still excluded from consideration, even though we now think we have passed beyond that heady and in many ways justified moment when it seemed that only Continental theory had the necessary force to displace the complacencies of our own tradition. The irony, of course, is that while looking to the Continent we failed to notice that Wilde has been and remains a very significant figure there. (And not only there: while the *Spectator* (February 1891) thought *The Soul of Man under Socialism* was a joke in bad taste, the essay soon became extremely successful in Russia, appearing in many successive editions across the next twenty years.) Perhaps, then, there exists or has existed a kind of 'muscular theory', which shares with the critical movements it has displaced a significant blindness with regard to Wilde and what he represented. This almost certainly has something to do with the persistence of an earlier attempt to rid English studies of a perceived 'feminized' identity.[64]

Recent critics of postmodernism, including Fredric Jameson, Ihab Hassan, Dan Latimer and Terry Eagleton,[65] have written intriguingly on one of its defining criteria: the disappearance of the depth model. In a recent essay, Eagleton offers an important and provocative critique of post-modernism: 'confidently post-metaphysical [it] has outlived all that fantasy of interiority, that pathological itch to scratch surfaces for concealed depths.' With the postmodern there is no longer any subject to be alienated and nothing to be alienated from, 'authenticity having been less rejected than merely forgotten'. The subject of postmodernist culture is 'a dispersed, decentred network of libidinal attachments, emptied of ethical substance and psychical interiority, the ephemeral function of this or that act of consumption, media experience, sexual relationship, trend or fashion'. Modernism, by contrast, is (or was) still preoccupied with the experience of alienation, with metaphysical depth and/or the psychic fragmentation and social wretchedness consequent upon the realization that there is no metaphysical depth or (this being its spiritual instantiation) authentic unified subject. As such, modernism is 'embarrassingly enmortgaged to the very bourgeois humanism it otherwise seeks to subvert'; it is 'a deviation still enthralled to a norm, parasitic on what it sets out to deconstruct'. But, concludes Eagleton, the subject of late capitalism is actually neither the 'self-regulating synthetic agent posited by classical humanist ideology, nor merely a decentred network of desire [as posited by postmodernism], but a contradictory amalgam of the two'. If in one respect the decentred, dispersed subject of postmodernism is suspiciously convenient to our own phase of late capitalism, it follows that those post-structuralist theorists who stake all on the assumption that the unified subject is still integral to contemporary bourgeois ideology, and that it is always a politically radical act to decentre and deconstruct that subject, need to think again.[66]

Eagleton's argument can be endorsed with yet further important distinctions. First, even though the unified subject was indeed an integral part of an earlier phase of bourgeois ideology, the instance of Gide and the tradition he represents must indicate that it was never even then exclusively in the service of dominant ideologies. Indeed, to the extent that Gide's essentialist legitimation of homosexual desire was primarily an affirmation of his own nature as pederast or paedophile, some critics might usefully rethink their own assumption that essentialism is fundamentally and always a conservative philosophy. In Gide we find essentialism in the service of a radical sexual nonconformity which was and remains incompatible with conventional and dominant sexual ideologies, bourgeois and otherwise. Even a glance at the complex and often contradictory histories of sexual liberation movements in our own time shows that they have, as does Eagleton's contradictory subject of late capitalism, sometimes and necessarily embraced a radical essentialism with regard to their own identity, while simultaneously offering an equally radical anti-essentialist critique of the essentializing sexual ideologies responsible for their oppression.

This is important: the implication of Eagleton's argument is not just that we need to make our theories of subjectivity a little more sophisticated, but rather that we need to be more historical in our practice of theory. Only then can we see the dialectical complexities of social process and social struggle. We may see, for example, how the very centrality of an essentialist concept to the dominant ideology has made its appropriation by a subordinate culture seem indispensable in that culture's struggle for legitimacy; roughly speaking, this corresponds to Gide's position as I am representing it here. The kind of challenge represented by Gide – liberation in the name of authenticity – has been more or less central to many progressive cultural struggles since, though it has not, of course, guaranteed their success.[67] Conversely, we may also see how other subordinate cultures and voices seek not to appropriate dominant concepts and values so much as to sabotage and displace them. This is something we can observe in Wilde.

Whether the decentred subject of contemporary post-structuralism and postmodernism is subversive of, alternative to, or actually produced by late capitalism, there is no doubt that Wilde's exploration of decentred desire and identity scandalized bourgeois culture in the 1890s and in a sense cost him his life. The case of Wilde might lead us to rethink the antecedents of postmodernism and, indeed, of modernism as they figure in the current debate which Eagleton addresses. Wilde prefigures elements of each, while remaining importantly different from – and not just obviously prior to – both. If his transgressive aesthetic anticipates postmodernism to the extent that it suggests a culture of the surface and of difference, it also anticipates modernism in being not just hostile to but intently concerned with its opposite, the culture of depth and exclusive integration. Yet Wilde's transgressive aesthetic differs from some versions of the postmodern in that it includes an acute political awareness and often an uncompromising political commitment; and his critique of the depth model differs from the modernist in that it is accompanied not by *Angst* but by something utterly different, something reminiscent of Barthes's *jouissance*, or what Borges has perceptively called Wilde's 'negligent glee . . . the fundamental spirit of his work [being] joy'.[68]

An anti-essentialist theory of subjectivity can in no way guarantee, *a priori*, any effect, radical or otherwise; nor, more generally, can any transgressive practice carry such a guarantee. But there is much to be learned retrospectively both from the effects of anti-essentialism and the practice of transgression, especially in the light of the currently felt need to develop new strategies and conceptions of resistance. Orthodox accounts of resistance have proved wanting, not least essentialist ideas of resistance in the name of the authentic self, and – in some ways the opposite – resistance in terms of and on behalf of mass movements working from outside and against the dominant powers. And so we have become acutely aware of the unavoidability of working from within the institutions that exist, adopting different strategies depending on where and who we are, or, in the case of the same individual, which subject positions s/he is occupying. But is this the new radicalism, or incorporation by another name?

It is in just these respects, and in relation to such pressing questions, that, far from finding them irrelevant – the one a *passé* wit and the other a *passé* moralist/essentialist – I remain intrigued with Wilde and Gide. In different ways their work explores what we are now beginning to attend to again: the complexities, the potential and the dangers of what it is to transgress, invert and displace *from within*;[69] the paradox of a marginality which is always interior to, or at least intimate with, the centre.

I began with their encounter in Algiers in 1895. Gide, dispirited in the sense of being depressed and unsure of himself, sees the names of Wilde and Douglas and erases his own name as a result, pre-empting perhaps the threat to his own identity, social and psychic, posed by Wilde's determination to demystify the normative ideologies regulating subjectivity, desire and the aesthetic. Nevertheless the meeting does occur, and Gide does indeed suffer an erasure of self, a decentring which is also the precondition for admitting transgressive desire, a depersonalization which is therefore also a liberation. Yet, for Gide, transgression is embraced with that same stubborn integrity which was to become the basis of his transgressive aesthetic, an aesthetic obviously indebted, yet also formed in reaction to, Wilde's own. Thus liberation from the self into desire is also to realize a new and deeper self, belief in which supports an oppositional stand not just on the question of deviant sexual desire, but on a whole range of other issues as well, cultural and political. Integrity here becomes an ethical sense inextricably bound up with and also binding up the (integral) unified self.[70] So the very categories of identity which, through transgression, Wilde subjects to inversion and displacement are reconstituted by Gide for a different transgressive aesthetic, or, as it might now more suitably be called in contradistinction to Wilde, a transgressive ethic: one which becomes central to the unorthodoxy which characterizes his life's work. In 1952, the year after his death, his entire works were entered in the Roman Catholic Index of Forbidden Books; six years earlier he had been awarded the Nobel Prize for Literature.

Wilde's fate was very different. Within weeks of returning from Algiers to London he was embroiled in the litigation against Queensberry which was to lead to his own imprisonment. He died in Paris in 1900, three years after his release. So, whereas Gide lived for fifty-seven years after that 1895 encounter, Wilde survived for only six. And yet it was also Wilde's fate to become a legend. Like many legendary figures, he needs to be rescued from most of his admirers and radically rethought by some, at least, of his critics.

University of Sussex

NOTES

Thanks to Joseph Bristow for his comments on an earlier draft of this paper.

1 André Gide, *If It Die* (1920; private edn 1926), trans. Dorothy Bussy (Harmondsworth: Penguin, 1977), p. 271.
2 Ibid., pp. 271, 273.
3 Jean Delay, *The Youth of André Gide*, abridged and trans. J. Guicharnaud (Chicago and London: University of Chicago Press, 1956–7), p. 290.
4 Richard Ellmann (ed.), *The Artist as Critic: Critical Writings of Oscar Wilde* (1968; London: W. H. Allen, 1970), p. xviii. Those aspects of Wilde's transgressive aesthetic which concern me here derive mainly from work published across a relatively short period of time, the years 1889–91. My reading of Wilde is avowedly partial. There is, of course, more – much more – to be said; about these works, about different works not discussed here, about

Wilde himself, especially about other of his ideas which intersect with and contradict the perspective explored here. My concern, though, is to address aspects of his work which have been largely ignored. What Richard Ellmann said of Wilde nearly twenty years ago is still true today: he 'laid the basis for many critical positions which are still debated in much the same terms, and which we like to attribute to more ponderous names' (ibid., p. x). Thomas Mann compared Wilde with Nietzsche; Ellmann in 1968 added the name of Roland Barthes. In 1987 we could add several more; more constructive, though, will be the renewed interest in Wilde that is sure to be generated by the expected publication this year of Ellmann's major biography.

5 J. Guicharnaud (trans.), *Correspondence 1890–1942, André Gide – Paul Valéry* (1955), cited here from the abridged version, *Self-Portraits: The Gide/ Valéry Letters* (Chicago and London: University of Chicago Press, 1966), pp. 90, 92.

6 Delay, op. cit., p. 291.

7 André Gide, *Journals*, 4 vols (New York: Alfred A. Knopf, 1947–51).

8 Delay, op. cit., pp. 289, 90, 291, 295.

9 Richard Ellmann (ed.), *Oscar Wilde: A Collection of Critical Essays* (Englewood Cliffs, NJ: Prentice-Hall, 1969), p. 4.

10 Quoted from Delay, op. cit., p. 391 (my italics).

11 André Gide, *Oscar Wilde*, trans. Bernard Frechtman (New York: Philosophical Library, 1949).

12 Gide, *If It Die*, pp. 280, 281.

13 Ibid., pp. 236–7, 247–9, 251, 252, 255, 258–9.

14 Ibid., p. 264.

15 Delay, op. cit., p. 394.

16 Gide, *If It Die*, pp. 282, 284–5.

17 Oscar Wilde, *The Soul of Man under Socialism* (1891), reprinted in Ellmann (ed.), *The Artist as Critic*, pp. 256 (his italics), 286–8, 288.

18 Ibid., pp. 259, 268, 260, 267.

19 Matthew Arnold, *Culture and Anarchy* (1869; London: Smith Elder, 1891), p. 8.

20 Wilde, *The Soul of Man under Socialism*, pp. 261, 258.

21 Wilde reiterates this elsewhere: see Oscar Wilde, 'Pen, pencil and poison' (1889), in Ellmann (ed.), *The Artist as Critic*, p. 338; 'The critic as artist' (1890), in Ellmann (ed.), *The Artist as Critic*, p. 360. Cf. Ellmann's formulation of Wilde's position: 'since the established social structure confines the individual, the artist must of necessity ally himself with the criminal classes' (Ellmann (ed.), *Oscar Wilde*, p. 3).

22 See also Wilde, 'The critic as artist', p. 341; Wilde, *The Soul of Man under Socialism*, pp. 271–4.

23 Wilde, *The Soul of Man under Socialism*, pp. 273, 284–5, 286.

24 Oscar Wilde, 'Mr Froude's Blue Book' (1889), in Ellmann (ed.), *The Artist as Critic*, pp. 136–7.

25 Wilde, *The Soul of Man under Socialism*, p. 265.

26 Oscar Wilde, 'The decay of lying' (1889), in Ellmann (ed.), *The Artist as Critic*, p. 310, and 'The critic as artist', p. 382.

27 Wilde, *The Soul of Man under Socialism*, p. 284.

28 Ibid., p. 284.

29 Wilde, 'The decay of lying', p. 297.

30 Ibid., p. 305.

31 For example, Wilde, 'The critic as artist', pp. 394, 399.

32 Oscar Wilde, *The Picture of Dorian Gray* (1890–1; Harmondsworth: Penguin, 1949), p. 10.

33 Wilde, 'The critic as artist', pp. 343, 368.

34 Wilde, *The Soul of Man under Socialism*, p. 272 (my italics).

35 Wilde, 'The critic as artist', p. 356.

36 Oscar Wilde, 'A few maxims for the instruction of the overeducated', *The Complete Works*, with introduction by Vyvyan Holland (London and Glasgow: Collins, 1948), p. 1203.

37 Wilde, 'The decay of lying', pp. 292 and 305.

38 Ibid., p. 305.

39 Wilde, 'The critic as artist', p. 399.

40 Delay, op. cit., p. 438.

41 André Gide, *The Immoralist* (1902; Harmondsworth: Penguin, 1960), pp. 51, 90, 100.

42 Gide, *If It Die*, p. 298.

43 Delay, op. cit., p. 396.

44 Gide, *If It Die*, p. 299.

45 Delay, op. cit., p. 467.

46 Ibid., p. 407.

47 Gide, *Journals*, p. 338. Cf. ibid., pp. 371–6.

48 Oscar Wilde, *Phrases and Philosophies for the Use of the Young* (1894), in Ellmann (ed.), *The Artist as Critic*, pp. 433–4.

49 The attacks on Wilde after his trial frequently reveal that it is masculinity which felt most under threat from him, and which demanded revenge.

50 Wilde, 'The critic as artist', p. 393.

51 Ibid., p. 398.

52 Oscar Wilde, *The Importance of Being Earnest* (1894–9), ed. R. Jackson (London: Ernest Benn, 1980), p. 83 (my italics).

53 Wilde, *The Picture of Dorian Gray*, p. 29.

54 Ibid., pp. 158–9.

55 H. M. Hyde, *Oscar Wilde: A Biography* (1976; London: Methuen, 1982), p. 271.

56 Michel Foucault, *The History of Sexuality*, vol. 1: *An Introduction* (1978; New York: Vintage Books, 1980), p. 43.

57 H. M. Hyde, *The Trials of Oscar Wilde* (London: William Hodge, 1948), p. 12.

58 Oscar Wilde, *De Profundis* (1897), in *The Letters of Oscar Wilde* (London: Rupert Hart-Davis, 1962); cited from the abridged edition, *Selected Letters* (London: Oxford University Press, 1979), p. 194. In certain important respects, *De Profundis* is a conscious renunciation by Wilde of his transgressive aesthetic. This is a work which registers many things, not least Wilde's courage and his despair during imprisonment. It also shows how he endured the intolerable by investing suffering with meaning, and this within a confessional narrative whose aim is a deepened self-awareness: 'I could not bear [my sufferings] to be without meaning. Now I find hidden somewhere away in my nature something that tells me that nothing in the whole world is meaningless . . . that something . . . is Humility.' Such knowledge and such humility, for Wilde (and still, for us now), is bought at the cost of fundamentally – deeply – renouncing difference and transgression and the challenge they present. In effect, Wilde repositions himself as the authentic, sincere subject which before

he had subverted: 'The supreme vice is shallowness,' he says in this work, and he says it more than once. And later: 'The moment of repentance is the moment of initiation' (ibid., pp. 195, 154, 215). This may be seen as that suffering into truth, that redemptive knowledge which points beyond the social to the transcendent realization of self, so cherished within idealist culture; those who see *De Profundis* as Wilde's most mature work often interpret it thus. I see it differently – as tragic, certainly, but tragic in the materialist sense of the word: a defeat of the marginal and the oppositional of a kind which only ideological domination can effect; a renunciation which is experienced as voluntary and self-confirming but which is in truth a self-defeat and a self-denial massively coerced through the imposition, by the dominant, of incarceration and suffering and their 'natural' medium, confession. What Wilde says here of the law is true also of the dominant ideologies he transgressed: 'I . . . found myself constrained to appeal to the very things against which I had always protested' (ibid., p. 221).

59 Foucault, op. cit., p. 101.
60 Jacques Derrida, *Positions* (London: 1981), pp. 41–2.
61 C. Baldick, *The Social Mission of English Criticism 1848–1932* (Oxford: Clarendon, 1983), pp. 213–18 (my italics).
62 I. A. Richards, quoted in ibid., p. 215.
63 Ibid., p. 217.
64 B. Doyle, 'The hidden history of English studies', in Peter Widdowson (ed.), *Re-Reading English* (London: Methuen, 1982); Terry Eagleton, *Literary Theory: An Introduction* (Oxford: Blackwell, 1983); Baldick, op. cit. On Wilde in Germany see Manfred Pfister (ed.), Oscar Wilde, *The Picture of Dorian Gray* (München: Wilhelm Fink, 1986).
65 Fredric Jameson, 'Postmodernism and consumer society', in H. Foster (ed.), *The Anti-Aesthetic: Essays on Postmodern Culture* (Washington, DC: Bay Press, 1983); Fredric Jameson, 'Postmodernism, or the cultural logic of late capitalism', *New Left Review*, 146 (1984); Ihab Hassan, 'Pluralism in postmodern perspective', *Critical Inquiry*, 12, 3 (1986), pp. 503–20; Dan Latimer, 'Jameson and postmodernism', *New Left Review*, 148 (1984), pp. 116–28; Terry Eagleton, 'Capitalism, modernism and postmodernism', in *Against the Grain* (London: Verso, 1986), pp. 131–47.
66 Eagleton, 'Capitalism, modernism and postmodernism', pp. 143, 132, 145, 143–5.
67 M. Berman, *The Politics of Authenticity: Radical Individualism and the Emergence of Modern Society* (London: Allen & Unwin, 1971).
68 Ellmann (ed.), *Oscar Wilde*, p. 174.
69 See Jacques Derrida, *Of Grammatology* (1967), trans. Gayatri Spivak (Baltimore, Md, and London: Johns Hopkins University Press, 1976), pp. lxxvi–lxxviii; Derrida, *Positions*, pp. 41–2; R. Terdiman, *Discourse/Counter Discourse: Theory and Practice of Symbolic Resistance in Nineteenth-Century France* (Ithaca, NY: Cornell University Press, 1985), esp. Introduction. Some of the most informative work addressing inversion and transgression is historically grounded; I have in mind especially recent work on early modern England. See, for example, D. Kunzle, 'World turned upside down: the iconography of a European broadsheet type', in Barbara Babcock (ed.), *The Reversible World: Symbolic Inversion in Art and Society* (Ithaca, NY, and London: Cornell University Press, 1978); Christopher Hill, *The World Turned Upside Down: Radical Ideas during the English Revolution* (Harmondsworth: Penguin,

1975); P. Stallybrass and A. White, *The Politics and Poetics of Transgression* (London: Methuen, 1986); S. Clark, 'Inversion, misrule and the meaning of witchcraft', *Past and Present*, 87 (1980), pp. 98–127. Kunzle, discussing the iconography of the world turned upside-down broadsheets, offers a conclusion which registers the complex potential of inversion and is, quite incidentally, nicely suggestive for understanding Wilde: 'Revolution appears disarmed by playfulness, the playful bears the seed of revolution. "Pure" formal fantasy and subversive desire, far from being mutually exclusive, are two sides of the same coin' (op. cit., p. 89). This is the appropriate point at which to note that the fuller study to which this article is a contribution necessarily address other considerations in relation to transgression in Wilde and Gide, most especially those of class race and colonialism. A crucial text for the latter is Gide's *Travels in the Congo* (1927–8), trans. D. Bussy (Harmondsworth: Penguin, 1986). But see also Jean-Paul Sartre, *What is Literature?* (1948; London: Methuen, 1967), esp. pp. 52, 98–9, 133.

70 It is instructive to see in Gide's writing how complex, vital and unconventional the existential and humanist commitment to sincerity of self could be, especially when contrasted with its facile counterpart in English studies, or indeed (a counter-image) the reductive ways in which it is sometimes represented in literary theory. See especially the following entries in Gide's *Journals*: 21 December and detached/recovered pages for 1923; January 1925; 7 October and 25 November 1927; 10 February (especially) and 8 December 1929; 5 August and September 1931; 27 June 1937.

LUDMILLA JORDANOVA

The popularization of medicine: Tissot on Onanism

Popularization has been surprisingly little studied by historians of science and medicine.[1] Indeed, it remains unclear just what popularization is and hence what approach best suits its investigation. Yet the proliferation of works which can only be described as 'popular' on scientific and medical subjects during the Enlightenment is a significant historical and literary phenomenon. While it would be possible to present 'popularization' as a simple spin-off of economic expansion and social mobility, the notion would then lose historical particularity, with the result that the *content* of such books becomes relatively uninteresting. Important questions remain: who wrote these works, for whom and why, what kind of a process is 'popularization'? The very idea of 'popularization' is problematic, since it apparently confirms an unfortunate dualism, with 'knowledge' and those who produce it on one side, and a diluted form of that knowledge and those who are its consumers on the other. One way of overcoming the consequences of a way of thinking that reinforces a schism between science/medicine and society is to treat scientific and medical texts as literature, and not to worry about their epistemological status. It is then possible to examine different genres, styles and textual strategies in a way that respects the unity and openness of eighteenth-century culture, the enormous interplay between areas we hold separate. Medical writings participate fully in larger trends, and there is an aspect of eighteenth-century 'popularization' that is particularly relevant here: the profound didacticism which so much medical writing of the period shares with literary productions on other subjects.

Popular medical works in the eighteenth century do not consciously seek to expound the results of 'research'. Frequently addressed to specific social groups (women, mothers, families, people with a particular social status or occupation), they generally address, advise and exhort the reader in some way. It does not follow from this that they are highly simplified. Indeed, there were wide variations in the amount of technical or linguistic knowledge presupposed. There seems to have been a degree of unity in their subject matter in that the relation of 'lifestyle' to health was mostly the central issue. I would suggest that this in part reflects the widespread continuing commitment of notions of constitution and temperament, the importance of habit and regimen, and the impact of the environment on health.[2] Consequently self-help and the prevention of disease occupy a prominent place.

In addition to the explicit advice given, numerous implicit assumptions were made about the social value of good health and about the social, even political consequences of illness. The idea of 'lifestyle' as embodied in eighteenth-century medical texts is, in fact, rather complex and was developed in a number of different ways. It could be a way of speaking about class, gender or even whole nations, as in the growing concern in the second half of the century with generating an adequate population to underpin the strength of the state.[3] Since medical advice books were sold to individuals, they consider the relationship between their readers and the larger social fabric as a matter of course. This is an important point, because they had to hold together a sense of individuals' responsibility for their own health and of the tangible effects of their wellbeing on others. The presentation of health in terms of selfhood is particularly striking. To be healthy was to have a competent, coherent identity; to be ill was to have fallen into a state which was somehow less than fully human.

Didactic literature proliferated in the eighteenth century. Several scholars who have studied general conduct books have noted their popularity, their tendency to re-use well-established and successful models, and the ways in which they were closely related to other forms of literature, often being formed by rearranging excerpts from publications of quite different kinds.[4] Medical advice books should thus be seen in the larger context of conduct books in general. It would be easy to suggest rather general explanations for the increased output of such literature: concern about social mobility, anxiety on the part of the mobile themselves, attempts to assert control by groups seeking to establish or maintain hegemony, the social ambitions of the writers who produced them, and so on. The present article has an altogether more modest aim: to examine more closely the form and content of such publications through a study of one in particular.

Surveys of broad categories of popular literature run the risk of neglecting the actual strategies that writers employed and the nature of the reading experience they offered their audiences. Of course, it would be naïve to suppose that we can ever reconstruct that experience. For one thing, we do not know how these works were used. Were they read from cover to cover, dipped into only when needed, or even bought to impress and never read at all? Furthermore, which family members read them? Were the numerous books addressed to mothers about female and childhood complaints really read by the women themselves? The questions are endless. Snippets of information about such matters can be gleaned from diaries and private papers, but these are, by their very nature, both fragmentary and unreliable.[5] Careful study of these texts can, however, tell us quite a lot about the audience constructed by the author, about the language of health and illness, and about the rhetorical strategies deemed most appropriate to the subject.

I propose to analyse only one such text, in order to illustrate how it works at many different levels, developing a complex, even contradictory role for the reader. This work can safely be designated as 'popular' in the most basic sense. It was clearly commercially successful, enjoying numerous eighteenth-century editions and being translated from the original Latin into French, English, Dutch, Italian and German.[6] I refer to Tissot's famous, or rather notorious, book on masturbation – a work which has been credited with having exercised enormous influence on attitudes towards sexuality over a considerable period of time. Be that as it may, it is, in my opinion, an extraordinary piece of *writing*. At this point it may be objected that such a work is not 'typical'. This may be true, but then searching for the 'typical' can be a misconceived and fruitless activity. None the less, it may be helpful to point to two characteristics of the book which are unusual. First, the presence of the author is exceptionally powerful. Often books of this kind are multi-authored, comprising extracts from existing works, or the identity of the writer was relatively unimportant. Second, and directly related to this, is Tissot's prominence in the medical and literary worlds of his day. He published on a wide range of controversial topics, including smallpox inoculation, plague, the people's health, fevers, epilepsy and nervous diseases. Many of the major figures of the Enlightenment were among his friends.[7] By contrast, many eighteenth-century medical advice books were written by provincial practitioners, who lacked the public prominence that Tissot enjoyed.

While it would be fallacious to suppose that simple norms exist in medicine, themes and strategies used by Tissot appear in other contemporary works, and many of his preoccupations are quite simply commonplaces in popular medical literature. There are, in fact, many extraordinary pieces of medical writing, although, like unhappy families, each is extraordinary in its own way. I make no apology, then, for choosing a single work, or for working here with a single edition, chosen purely for convenience. It is the one printed in Dublin in 1772, translated from the French by 'A. Hume M.D.', the translator of the English editions and himself an author of a medical advice book, *Every Woman her own Physician; or, the Lady's Medical Assistant* (London, 1776).

An Essay on Onanism, or a Treatise upon the Disorders produced by Masturbation: or the Dangerous Effects of Secret and Excessive Venery is a work often referred to but seldom read. It is written in an almost autobiographical mode, full of references to people Tissot knows or has corresponded with, anecdotes he has heard about, and his own clinical experiences. Since the author's presence is established both strongly and informally, Tissot can address the reader directly, as in a conversation, yet with authority. Needless to say, however, in the course of 150 pages cataloguing self-inflicted woes, he appeals to other kinds of authorities. Many of these are major medical sources from the seventeenth and earlier eighteenth centuries; others are classical, ranging from the expected use of

Galen and Hippocrates to the more surprising invocation of literary sources like Horace and Plutarch, who are quoted in Latin. When coupled with the conversational style, this gives the 'information' conveyed, at least to our eyes, a variety of epistemological statuses. They range from 'I have seen myself . . .' to 'Someone has written to tell me that he has heard/seen . . .', and include the standard citations of respected authors like Harvey, Boerhaave and Haller. Constant movement between these levels enables Tissot to relate endless individual case histories, sometimes about named or identifiable people. This certainly serves to heighten a sense of drama about health which Tissot appears to cultivate knowingly. Many of the cases he recounts end in death, and thus embody all the features of a moral fable. The overt lessons to be learned are unambiguous, simple and unoriginal. At heart there is only one lesson, 'moderation', a notion that dominates not just medical but the vast majority of didactic writings in the eighteenth century. Moderation implies self-control, and where the 'self' is not up to the task, as with children, the control must be exercised by others. The moral tales in Tissot's *Essay* are thus addressed to a variety of audiences – the young, parents, guardians, other medical practitioners and also possibly the 'general reader'.

Thus far, the special nature of the subject matter has not been mentioned, yet this dominates the book as it has dominated its reception.[8] It discusses that which is not normally discussed; it penetrates the secret lives of those whose stories are told and, by implication, those who read it. Not only does it speak, at length, about things unmentionable, but it does so specifically in relation to a group of people for whom the implications are particularly shocking – children. Tissot's text establishes the existence of the sexuality of children, implies the need for its control, and argues that failure to curb it has permanent consequences because of the peculiar damage done by loss of such an important entity as the seminal fluid before maturity is attained.[9]

We may reasonably suppose that children themselves did not read Tissot. None the less, with an adult audience in mind, he acknowledged the difficulty of finding the right language.

> I can venture to aver that I have not neglected any precaution that was necessary to give this work all the decency, in point of terms, that it was susceptible of. . . . Should such important subjects be passed over in silence? No, certainly. The sacred writers, the fathers of the church, who almost all wrote in living languages, the ecclesiastical writers, did not think it proper to be silent upon crimes of obscenity, because they could not be described without words. . . . I hope to deserve the acknowledge- ment and approbation of virtuous and enlightened men, who are acquainted with the proneness of men to evil. (p. iv)

Tissot thereby simultaneously claims the right to speak on 'indecent' matters, and models his discourse on that of the church. While there are many differences between his approach and a theological one, his invocation of the example of the early church fathers is none the less interesting. It allows him to introduce quasi-religious notions of evil and sin which can be coupled with the naturalistic arguments against sexual excess. Furthermore, it fits well with the confessional tone of much of the work. Case histories often take the following form: a patient has some symptoms, attempts are made to treat them to no avail, the patient is invited to confess his secret indulgences, whereupon the true causes of his plight are known. Either death or recovery can follow. Here, the medical practitioner indeed takes on a priestly role, arrogating to himself the right to pry, to know and to pass judgement on a secret existence. The demand to know about the sexuality of others by requiring them to give an account of themselves, which Foucault has written about, is thus well established in Tissot.[10]

A further issue is raised by the problem of finding an appropriate language for sexuality. Perhaps the analogy of witchcraft is useful here. There is considerable historical evidence that in some parts of Europe witch-hunts developed as a result of élite obsessions with the power of the devil, and that they accelerated with the use of torture, which encouraged people to denounce each other.[11] As a result, it becomes impossible for historians to give an account of witchcraft itself. Rather they must perforce study discourses about witchcraft, brought into existence by the interaction of different groups. It was the speaking and writing about magic that was important, not the acts they purported to describe. Perhaps the same can be said about sexuality. In writing about Tissot, several historians have likened him to a witch-hunter in order to blame him retrospectively for persecuting innocent victims. I agree that the analogy is a useful one, not because we should pass judgement on him, but because it highlights the fact that it was reading, writing and speaking about the forbidden that was an issue in both cases. The similarities go further; Tissot gave a voice to that which was 'unmentionable', just as the witch-hunters had.[12] Both 'persecutor' and 'persecuted' had to speak the same language, enter into the same universe of meaning. Tissot and others were engaged in constructing elaborate discourses which, while they purported to condemn a whole range of irresponsible activities, in fact also celebrated them in words, by giving them a language, a vocabulary, an audience, a significance.

Just as the persecution of witchcraft allowed, indeed encouraged, the recounting of sexually transgressive activities, so Tissot permitted the relentless cataloguing of 'crimes' and positively enjoyed offering gruesome details. There is no inherent limit to these recitations, and endless elaborations can be introduced. As subordinate clauses can be added to sentences, so extra examples and further details could be added to Tissot's accounts. Discourses about sexuality can proliferate promiscuously. An example of Tissot's celebratory approach will perhaps illustrate these points.

> I was called upon, Feb. 10, 1760, to pay a visit in the country to a man, about forty years of age, who had been of a very strong and robust constitution; but who had been guilty of great excesses with women and

wine, and who had greatly exerted himself in what may be stiled [*sic*] remarkable feats of that kind. [Tissot then offers a vivid description of the man's symptoms.]

It appeared to me that the original cause of the disorder was too free an use of women and wine; and I thought that the feats which he had often performed might be the cause of the muscles being more particularly affected. (p. 35)

Tissot's writing contains two contrary positions here: at an explicit level a cautionary tale is beginning in which a sinner will get his just deserts, but the repetition of his exploits together with the use of the word 'feats', which titillates the reader and invites him or her to speculate about just what these 'feats' could be, indicates a rather different moral stance. On the one hand Tissot wants to argue that too much sexual activity makes people ill, and to make a convincing, persuasive case for this through his vivid use of language, while on the other hand the pleasure he derives from writing about sexuality at length is also apparent.

Such an ambivalence goes deep into the structure of the book, and we can see it quite clearly if we return for a moment to the issue of childhood sexuality.

A child of this city [Montpellier], at the age of between six and seven, instructed, as I imagine, by a servant maid, polluted himself so often, that a slow fever, which succeeded, finished him. His rage for this act was so great, that he could not be restrained from it the very last days of his life. When he was informed that he thereby hastened his death, he consoled himself, in saying, that he should the sooner meet with his father, who died some months before. (p. 23)

Here is a child consumed with sexual passion, yet capable of fine sentiments. Moreover, his habit came not from within himself, but from an external agent of a different, lower social class. In order to offer a general explanation for the devastating effects of masturbation, Tissot turns to the nature of seminal fluid itself, and attributes to it formidable vital powers: 'the loss of an ounce of this humour would weaken more than that of forty ounces of blood' (p. 10). We can also apprehend the potency of 'seminal liquor' by the far-reaching physical changes that take place during male puberty and, conversely, as a result of castration. It is thus *possible* for Tissot to explain his pathological observations in physiological terms.

However, when it comes to particular cases of children, he stresses the role of external agents to give a *social* account of the problem's origin. This is the advice he offers to parents on the subject of servants and preceptors. I quote the passage in full in order to convey the range of metaphors Tissot employs:

I could produce but too great a number of young plants, who have been lost by the very gardener who was instructed with their rearing. There are in this kind of culture, gardeners of both sexes. But I shall be asked where is the remedy to this evil? The answer is within my sphere, and I shall give it in a concise manner. Be particularly careful in the choice of a preceptor, watch over him and his pupil with that vigilance, which an attentive and enlightened father of a family exerts to know what is done in the darkest recesses of his house; use that vigilance which discovers the coppice where the deer has taken shelter, when it has escaped all other eyes: this is always possible when it is earnestly pursued. . . . Never leave young people alone with their masters, if these are suspected; and prevent their having any correspondence with the servants. (p. 43)[13]

There is an undertow of violence here which is all the more striking for the contrast between the idea of children as plants, which is common at this time (Rousseau's *Émile* is one of the best-known examples), and the idea of the father as a hunter. Likening children to plants can serve a variety of purposes, such as evoking a sense of latency, but generally it presents them as passive, adaptive and malleable, easily trained.[14] The hunting image is not only more violent, but contains movement, terror and persecution. But who or what is the father hunting? Is it the masturbating child, the corrupting tutor or sexuality itself that the deer stands for? Yet the father is more than this: he is also to become an all-seeing eye or a beam of light which dispels darkness, and with it the privacy of the child. Tissot's solution to the 'problem' of childhood sexuality lies not in medicine but in the social arrangements of the household.

That Tissot's concerns are more social-cum-moral than strictly medical is amply borne out by his treatment of other themes. Furthermore, he conceives the issue of the control of sexuality in terms of individual responsibility. We can see this in the fact that, concerned though he is with masturbation in adolescent boys, Tissot condemns *all* excessive sex, even within marriage. Individuals who indulge themselves sexually are taking the first step on the road to suicide (see p. 5, for instance). In addition, Tissot repeatedly stresses the melancholy of afflicted individuals, and melancholy is pre-eminently the disease of the self-absorbed; it is a recurrent theme of the literature on masturbation. In his edition of Tissot, the early nineteenth-century French hygienist Hallé nicely turns this association around by claiming that it is *reading* Tissot that induces melancholy![15]

When Tissot comes to list the reprehensible habits likely to get the young into trouble, they are all associated with a self-indulgent, luxurious lifestyle: 'idleness and inactivity, lying too long a-bed, over soft beds, succulent aromatics, salt and vinous diet, suspicious friends, licentious productions . . . should sedulously be avoided' (p. 124). Narcissism seems to be the trouble. There are passages where, to get his point across, Tissot launches into a description of symptoms which constitutes a verbal attack of some force, where he revels in the power of his own words:

A description of the danger to a person who is addicted to the evil, is perhaps the most powerful motive of correction. It is a dreadful portrait sufficient to make him retreat with horror. . . . The whole mass fallen to decay; all the bodily senses and all the faculties of the soul weakened; the loss of imagination and memory; and imbecility, contempt, shame, ignominy, its constant attendants; . . . the humiliating character of being an useless load upon earth; the mortification to which it is daily exposed, a distaste for all decent pleasures; lassitude, an aversion for others, and at length for self; life appears horrible; the dread which every moment starts at suicide; anguish worse than pain; remorse. (p. 126)

There is a relentlessness about Tissot's description which suggests an element of pleasure derived from the recounting of pain and misery in others. This prose displays one of the characteristics of discourses on sexuality identified earlier: it is potentially infinite, since more and more examples can be piled on top of one another. Even the sentence structure and punctuation confirm this. But more interesting is the *content* of Tissot's description-cum-denunciation.

By turning his attention inwards, the masturbator disintegrates as an individual self and as a social being. 'Useless load' is a term for social nonexistence or, perhaps worse, for dependence upon others. Tissot's elaborate descriptions, case studies, anecdotes, quotations and stories amount to a definition of health and its preservation in terms of the correct form of selfhood. In childhood, total control will be exercised over the child so that his relationships with social inferiors in particular are mediated through the father. At a symbolic level, Tissot develops the idea of a precious gift being husbanded; parents patrol children to prevent profligacy. This sets in place the habits which, for the rest of an individual's life, act as a kind of guarantee that excessive introspection and self-indulgence will not take place. To do otherwise is to lose one's self, and hence to lose social legitimation, the consequences of the self-regarding dispersal of the most vital of vital fluids. It is ironic that Rousseau, according to Lejeune, also associated masturbation with introspection, but not in Tissot's sense.[16] Rather, for Rousseau, it was related to the creative imagination and reverie. Yet in *Émile* he condemns it, in terms very like those of Tissot, whom he admired.

We cannot, of course, know just how widespread were these views that ill-health and loss of selfhood were two facets of the same coin. Many medical advice books rehearse similar arguments, even if relatively few of them develop such powerful images. Similarly, philanthropic and reformist literature of the period manifests precisely these concerns. Two examples spring to mind: writings about the reform of prostitutes, which concentrate on re-establishing self-control and self-esteem; and attacks on homosexuality, which often register fears about the loss of individual and class identity.[17]

What links these areas together is the notion of 'unnatural acts'. These may be understood as activities which threaten to rob people of their fully human status, by making them closer to animals, or by degrading them into helplessness or dependence Yet this notion of the 'unnatural' is deeply problematic in an era noted by many scholars as one in which the commitment to sex as part of the natural order is particularly strong. Hence the boundary between 'natural' and 'unnatural' had to be negotiated with care. I would suggest that this was achieved partly through a distinction between productive and unproductive sex. By this I do not simply mean procreative or non-procreative sex, although that is involved. Rather, 'productive' here conveys a sense of those sexual activities which have positive outcomes for individuals and for society as a whole. Those who render themselves mentally, physically and socially incompetent through masturbation are clearly indulging in unproductive sex. By contrast, a married couple enjoying moderate sex, even if conception rarely results, would be an example of those who use their sexuality productively and responsibly.

Tissot was particularly concerned that young people who masturbated would be disinclined to marry – a concern which also features in the contemporary literature on prostitution. Celibacy and sterility were feared consequences – according to Tissot, especially for women. This demonstrates how profound were commitments to gender *difference*. Here, as elsewhere, gender offered a language through which wider issues could be explored. For example, denunciations of male homosexuality in this period often speak of 'effeminacy' and 'degeneracy'. Tissot, by contrast, associates female homosexuality with the usurpation of a masculine role. It is notable that when discussing the effects of masturbation on women he moves so 'naturally' to the question of homosexuality. He attacks homosexual women on two grounds. First, he associates lesbianism with deformed genitalia – that is, with monstrosity. Second, he accuses them of being over-masculine: 'some women who were thus imperfect, glorying, perhaps, in this kind of resemblance, seized upon the functions of virility' (pp. 44–5). In effect, it was being stated that two complementary, that is to say, distinct yet related beings were a necessary precondition for 'natural' sexual relations to take place. While these manœuvres might work quite well in relation to the sexuality of adults, it was much harder to sustain them in relation to children, because children were so frequently taken as a paradigm of 'the natural'.[18] If sex was natural and children equally so, then an activity so often associated with children would seem to qualify for that epithet too. To resist this implication also involved some elaborate reconceptualizations.

We have already noted one of the ways in which Tissot does this, namely by identifying an external agent, often of a lower social class than the child, as the cause of corruption.[19] He also believes in the importance of education in the regulation of 'natural' propensities. Human nature, if it is not to be too disruptive, needs moulding in the correct forms. Here Tissot is in line with so many of his contemporaries, as he is too in the way in which he thinks about this moulding, educative process as one that internalizes moral norms. In children the process is incomplete. Yet it must be achieved if they are to become adults who are not socially dependent (for example, through ill health) or too self-absorbed, both of which conditions lead to inadequate development, signalled by poor health. Autonomy without narcissism, social relations without dependence, were his goals. Tissot thus defines health in terms of a particular kind of self, one that is not self-indulgent and hence has that degree of self-control which allows it to function in society. There is a further implication: the location where such healthy selves are constructed is 'the family', an abstraction than can simultaneously hold a belief in sexuality as part of nature and have a commitment to its moral regulation for social ends. While clearly not all health problems raised the particularly tricky problems that masturbation did, most of them could be related to questions of lifestyle, habit, constitution and temperament which, in turn, suggest precisely the same issues about the healthy self and its conditions of existence, as well as about its intimate relations with other selves, particularly within the family.[20]

Like other medical authors of so-called advice books, Tissot presented means by which control could be successfully internalized, and, like them, he deluged the reader with a turbulent, conflict-ridden barrage of prose that created powerful images of adequacy and inadequacy, a dichotomy which related to gender, nature and the family, and which, above all, differentiated 'natural' from 'unnatural' development. At the same time, his text suggests the special pleasures to be derived from talking about forbidden topics. It is misleading to attribute to Tissot a reorientation of attitudes about masturbation and sexuality away from religion and towards medicine. Although he takes health as a major criterion of judgement, the medical focus is far from exclusive. In fact it is his *inclusiveness* which is striking. Notions of sin, evil, crime and punishment are all incorporated into a larger vision, which sets improper sexual activity in the context of class relations, family dynamics, responsibility and dependency, allowing him to move effortlessly between individual and social identity. Tissot shifts equally easily between patients' observable symptoms and their attitudes, feelings and unseen behaviour. There is a further blurring here of internal and external, of subjective and objective.

If it seems worthwhile to examine popular medical books as examples of particular kinds of discourses, a number of implications follow. First, we should be more attentive to the rich language of such writings; historians might do well to turn to literary criticism for useful models. Second, if specific examples of popular writing achieved prominence in the past, an explanation of this in terms of their literary power may be more helpful than supposing, for example, that they cater to contemporary 'neuroses'.[21] Third, if the metaphors of medicine are constitutive of the ideas and theories of practitioners, then textual analysis must become a central historical tool. Fourth, since the writing itself has embedded within it a whole host of social preoccupations and tensions, understanding its language reveals how world-views are both confirmed and called into question. And, finally, focusing on language helps us avoid the unfortunate dualism of most treatments of 'popularization', since language constitutes the common cultural core, which is no less fundamental to the science and medicine of the Enlightenment than it is to 'literature' as conventionally defined.

University of Essex

NOTES

1 See B. Ehrenreich and D. English (eds), *For Her Own Good: 150 Years of the Experts' Advice to Women* (London, Pluto, 1979); C. Lawrence, 'William Buchan: medicine laid open', *Medical History*, 19 (1975), pp. 20–35; R. Porter (ed.), *Patients and Practitioners: Lay Perceptions of Medicine in Pre-Industrial Society* (Cambridge, University Press 1985); J. A. Secord, 'Newton in the nursery: Tom Telescope and the philosophy of tops and balls, 1761–1838'. *History of Science*, 23 (1985), pp. 127–51; T. Shinn and R. Whitley (eds), *Expository Science: Forms and Functions of Popularisation* (Dordrecht, Reidel 1985).

2 See G. Smith, 'Prescribing the rules of health: self-help and advice in the late eighteenth century', in Porter (ed.), op. cit., pp. 249–82.

3 P. Buck, 'People who counted: political arithmetic in the eighteenth century', *Isis*, 73 (1982), pp. 28–45; J. S. Taylor, 'Philanthropy and empire: Jonas Hanway and the infant poor of London', *Eighteenth-Century Studies*, 12 (1979), pp. 285–305.

4 See L. A. Curtis, 'A case study of Defoe's domestic conduct manuals suggested by *The Family, Sex and Marriage in England 1500–1800'*, *Studies in Eighteenth Century Culture*, 10 (1981), pp. 409–28; K. Hornbeak, 'Richardson's *Familiar Letters* and the domestic conduct books', *Smith College Studies in Modern Languages*, 19 (1938), pp. 1–29; R. Paulson, *Popular and Polite Art in the Age of Hogarth and Fielding* (Notre Dame University Press, 1979), pt. 2, ch. 3.

5 See L. Beier, 'In sickness and in health: a seventeenth century family's experience', in Porter (ed.), op. cit., pp. 101–28; J. Lane, 'The doctor scolds me: the diaries and correspondence of patients in eighteenth century England', in Porter (ed.), op. cit., pp. 205–48.

6 Although I know of no definitive bibliographical study of the numerous editions of Tissot's work, the catalogues of the British Library, the Wellcome Institute Library and the Library of Congress list many different editions. (The first edition was in Latin (Lausanne, 1758) and is quite rare.)

7 C. Eynard, *Essai sur la vie de Tissot* (Lausanne, 1839); P. Lejeune, 'Le "dangéreux supplément": lecture d'un aveu de Rousseau', *Annales*, 29 (1974), pp. 1009–22; G. Minder-Chappuis, 'Auguste Tissot: sa correspondance avec A. de Haller et ses œuvres durant la période de 1754 à 1761' (Berne, n.d.), unpublished dissertation presented to the Faculté de Médecine; T. Tarczylo, ' "Prêtons la main à la nature ..." *L'Onanisme de Tissot'*, *Dix-Huitième Siècle*, No. 12 (1980), pp. 79–96.

8 See P.-G. Boucé, 'Aspects of sexual tolerance and intolerance in eighteenth-century England', *British Journal for Eighteenth Century Studies*, 3 (1980), pp. 173–91; P.-G. Boucé (ed.), *Sexuality in Eighteenth Century Britain* (Manchester University Press, 1982); H. T. Engelhardt, 'The disease of masturbation: values and the concept of disease', *Bulletin of the History of*

Medicine, 48 (1974), pp. 234–48; E. H. Hare, 'Masturbatory insanity: the history of an idea', *Journal of Mental Science*, 108 (1962), pp. 1–25; A. McLaren, 'Some secular attitudes toward sexual behaviour in France 1760–1860', *French Historical Studies*, 8 (1973–4), pp. 604–25.

9 P. Ariès, *Centuries of Childhood* (Harmondsworth, Penguin Books, 1973); G. Boas, *The Cult of Childhood* (London, Warburg Institute 1966); J. H. Plumb, 'The new world of children in 18th century England', *Past and Present*, No. 67 (1975), pp. 64–95; L. Pollock, *Forgotten Children: Parent–Child Relations from 1500–1900* (Cambridge, University Press 1983).

10 M. Foucault, *The History of Sexuality*, vol. 1: *An Introduction* (London, Allen Lane 1979); cf. McLaren, op. cit.

11 S. Watts, *A Social History of Western Europe 1450–1720* (London, Hutchinson 1984), ch. 5; C. Merchant, *The Death of Nature* (London, Wildwood 1982), ch. 5; *History Today*, November 1980 and February 1981.

12 C. Belsey, *The Subject of Tragedy: Identity and Difference in Renaissance Drama* (London, Methuen 1985), pp. 185–91.

13 I have discussed this same passage in a different context in 'Naturalising the family: literature and the bio-medical sciences in the late eighteenth century', in L. Jordanova (ed.), *Languages of Nature: Critical Essays on Science and Literature* (London, Free Association Books 1986), p. 114.

14 Book I of *Émile* is full of such references. A less well-known example is W. Cadogan, *An Essay upon Nursing and the Management of Children from their Birth to Three Years of Age* (London, 1748).

15 Lejeune, op. cit., p. 1016.

16 Ibid., pp. 1020–2.

17 C. Jones, 'Prostitution and the ruling class in 18th century Montpellier', *History Workshop Journal*, 6 (1978), pp. 7–28; W. Speck, 'The Harlot's Progress in eighteenth-century England', *British Journal for Eighteenth Century Studies*, 3 (1980), pp. 127–39; A. Bray, *Homosexuality in Renaissance England* (London, Gay Men's Press 1982); R. Trumbach, 'London's sodomites: homosexual behaviour and Western culture in the eighteenth century', *Journal of Social History*, 11 (1977), pp. 1–33.

18 D. G. Charlton, *New Images of the Natural in France: A Study in European Cultural History 1750–1800* (Cambridge, University Press 1984), pp. 139–53.

19 C. Fairchilds, *Domestic Enemies: Servants and their Masters in Old Regime France* (Baltimore, Md, Johns Hopkins University Press 1984), ch. 7.

20 J. Donzelot, *The Policing of Families* (London, Hutchinson 1979); Foucault, op. cit.

21 R. H. MacDonald, 'The frightful consequences of onanism: notes on the history of a delusion', *Journal of the History of Ideas*, 28 (1967), p. 431.

ROGER POOLE

Midrash

- Geoffrey H. Hartman and Sanford Budick (eds), *Midrash and Literature* (New Haven, Conn., and London: Yale University Press, 1986), 412 pp., £27.50

The moment has finally come when the deconstructive enterprise has turned full circle and is now in quest of its own unwritten presuppositions. The time has come when deconstruction, its heady first triumphs of dismantling over, has returned in a quietened mood to examine what it has in common with more traditional interpretative and hermeneutic exercises.

Midrash and Literature might then be seen as the opening of Act II of the high drama which began in 1967 with Jacques Derrida's *De la grammatologie*. In 1967 all was dismantling, disclosure, stripping bare of metaphysical presuppositions. This brilliant enterprise was, of course, not without its cost. Expensively, grammatology did away with author, intention, 'meaning', reference and the 'metaphysics of presence'. In an exemplary reading of Lévi-Strauss, a *tour de force*, even the great anti-humanist himself was shown to be harbouring logocentric assumptions.

By the time Geoffrey Hartman came to write his two cadenzas on Derrida's *Glas* in *The Georgia Review* for 1976, Derrida himself seemed to have become the central text – which itself lay beyond any possible deconstruction. But with Hartman's seeming retraction in *Saving the Text* (1981) there was a sense that, for Hartman himself at least, one part of the enterprise had reached the limits of its viability. Hartman proposed at that time a founding, extratextual reality which should return to words their old ability to curse and to bless, to enrich and to impoverish human life, and also to mean and refer beyond themselves, to resonate with an importance quite beyond what their mere textual condition would seem to justify.

The second phase of deconstruction is, then, reconstitutive, interpretative, hermeneutic. Bare ruined quires are now being re-examined for any sanctity which may have escaped de-essentialization the first time round. Derrida now suggests that we have got to go back over our tracks and reread Husserl and Hegel with a phenomenological attention: not, obviously, one that precedes the discoveries of deconstruction, but one that follows and is aware of its lessons.

It is not surprising that it should be the author of *Saving the Text* who now, in collaboration with Sanford Budick, ushers into the world this very handsome volume from Yale University Press. It is obviously a collaboration which works at a very high level of intuitive sympathy, of common aims and perceptions. It is fitting too that a book that deals with the enduring qualities of sacred scriptures should be so magnificently produced. The paper used meets 'guidelines for permanence and durability'; the print is clear and fine and the essays beautifully written and presented. Each essayist, moreover, has profited from the excellent editorial practice of allowing collaborators to peruse each other's work before coming to a final recension of their own. It is a volume put together out of love, out of respect. It is a book which seems to call us, in some Heideggerian way, 'from afar', and Heidegger suggests that it is just because we were half awaiting the call that we recognize its significance.

It is worth starting from a definition of 'midrash', and where better to find one than in the glossary at the end of the book:

> MIDRASH: From the root meaning 'to seek out' or 'to inquire': a term in rabbinic literature for the interpretative study of the Bible. By extension the word is also used in two related senses: first, to refer to the results of that interpretative activity, namely, the specific interpretations produced through midrashic exegesis; and, second, to describe the literary compilations in which the original interpretations, many of them first delivered and transmitted orally, were eventually collected.

Midrash, then, is interpretation and commentary, and in the Introduction the editors point to 'the resemblances between midrash and highly similar critical phenomena which, for whatever reasons, have acquired central importance in contemporary literature, criticism and theory.' There are obviously also significant differences, and it is important to be aware of the nature of these. The most important is the fact that midrash does not operate on a secular text: 'Given the theological principles of divine univocity and inviolability of the sacred text there are . . . significant constraints and restraints upon the freedom of midrash.' There is a special 'joy of recognition' in the midrashic 'return to the prime text', and, precisely because there is a firm prime text to return to, the 'infinities of the Torah . . . abolish the category of the secondary'.

Another important aspect of midrash is its attention to the sheer physical givenness of the original text. Unlike Christian exegesis, which has to rely on translations, Joseph Dan explains,

> Jewish preachers could use a total text, hermeneutically discussing not only the meaning of terms and words, but also their sound, the shape of the letters, the vocalization points and their shapes and sounds . . . and the countless ways other than ideonic content and meaning by which the scriptures transmit a semiotic message.

The similarity of that close textual scrutiny and Derrida's technique is striking, and the one may yet turn out to have had far more to do with the other than we have hitherto suspected.

Each contributor has the freedom, inherent obviously in the practice of midrash itself, to define his subject as seems best to him. James Kugel writes:

> Suffice it to say that the Hebrew word *midrash* might be best translated as 'research', a translation that incorporates the word's root meaning of 'search out, inquire' and perhaps as well suggests that the results of that research are almost by definition recherché, that is, not obvious, out-of-the-way, sometimes far-fetched. . . . At bottom midrash is not a genre of interpretation but an interpretative stance, a way of reading the sacred text, and we shall use it in this broad sense. (p. 91)

It is beginning to become clear why midrash should be peculiarly suited to be taken up into the theoretical debate at this point. It is especially helpful in the interpretation of the *kind of text* that criticism currently finds most attractive – that is, texts which are anyway ambiguous and multi-layered, overdetermined or semantically 'undecidable'. It is not a surprise to see the names of Borges, Kafka, Célan and a text of Edmond Jabès at the end of the collection under the heading 'Contemporary midrash'. Not surprising, either, to find Frank Kermode starting from an enigmatic poem by Wallace Stevens in order to show us the difficulties involved in establishing 'The plain sense of things'.

Perhaps the most surprising presence at this latterday celebration of midrash is Defoe, but, in one of the best-written essays in the book, Harold Fisch shows again and again that 'The hermeneutic quest in *Robinson Crusoe* is deliberately carried out at a variety of levels: The story of Robinson's many trials on the island may be read as a kind of midrash on Jonah.' Not only that, but 'the question which he constantly asks himself is that of Moses, Job, Jonah, indeed all the heroes of the Bible: Why am I singled out?' Robinson's ability to survive on his island is entirely due to his own hermeneutic and midrashic talent, and this itself is an ability underwritten by a peculiarly practical reading of his Bible.

Hermeneutic ability can come in very handy, then. Fever-crazed, and fearing the recurrence of dreadful dreams, Crusoe remembers that 'in one of his chests he has a roll of tobacco-leaf used in Brazil as a medicine for all manner of ailments'. He opens his chest, finds the wonderful tobacco, and next to it a Bible, which falls open at Psalm 50: 'Call on me in the Day of Trouble, and I will deliver thee, and thou shalt glorify me.' Fisch elegantly binds together his interpretative instruments:

> The tobacco, it seems, is the material exemplification of the deliverance spoken of in that verse from Psalms. And the two, text and referent, are literally contiguous! Of course the two do not always rest comfortably side by side as in this instance. Sometimes the Book will supervene and sometimes the Tobacco. (p. 222)

It is perhaps lateral thinking of this kind that James Kugel was writing about when he referred to midrash as having results which are 'almost by definition recherché, that is, not obvious'. For the relation of psalm to tobacco is not in any way direct: it is not as a result of an act of interpretation, in our literary sense, that we could see the connection between psalm and tobacco, but by an act of connection. Midrash is partly the art of seeing connections where straight interpretation would not necessarily perceive (or allow) any. There is something parallel about this form of thinking, something which has to do with a perception trained in the study of double, triple or quadruple columns of writing down a page, something delicately re-produced in *Glas*.

It may be, then, that the intention of Geoffrey Hartman and Sanford Budick, in offering us a whole volume of applied studies on and in midrash, has to do with preparing us for a new type of interpretation, one which would not move only from the top of the page downwards, as it were, but from column to column, sideways. Maybe the suggestion is that interpretation, as such, is too limited by its own preconceptions of what is and what is not legitimate as an interpretative procedure. We recall, after all, the kind of problems raised by Julia Kristeva and Philippe Sollers in *Tel Quel* twenty years back, about whether a text could be literally infinite in its signifying ability, and the efforts of rather shocked custodians of the academic rulebook to establish some kind of bank-managerial limit to such a potential semantic overdraft. Suppose, then, that midrash makes that entire problem irrelevant by proposing new conventions for what does and what does not constitute an interpretation?

Reading through Jacques Derrida's own long essay on 'Shibboleth', for instance, an essay which is half about Célan and half about circumcision, we are forced (if we wish to follow the argument at all) to give up certain habits of mind about what would and what would not constitute a proper attentiveness to Derrida's mode of argument and to Célan's own texts. This, for example, is (I take it?) an example of midrash in action:

> A *Shibboleth*, the word *Shibboleth*, if it is one, names, in the broadest extension of its generality or its usage, any insignificant, arbitrary mark, for example the phonemic difference between *shi* and *si*, once it becomes discriminative and decisive, that is, divisive. The difference has no meaning in and of itself, and becomes what one must know how to mark or recognize if one is to *get on*, if, that is, one is to *get over* a border or the threshold of a poem, if one is to be granted asylum or the legitimate habitation of a language. And to inhabit a language, one must already have a *Shibboleth* at one's command: it is not enough simply to understand the meaning of the word, simply to *know* how it should be pronounced (*shi* and not *si*, this the Ephraimites knew). One must *be able* to say it as it should be said. There is nothing hidden about this secret, this claim of alliance, no meaning concealed within a crypt, but it is a cipher which one must *share and divide* (partager) with the other. (pp. 322–3)

Midrash, then, has much to do with inhabiting a tradition, knowing how to *get on* in a tradition, knowing how to fend for oneself among apparently strange scriptural events. It has to do with survival, with wit, with getting the joke, picking up the reference, perceiving the similarity. It has to do with what we partly know beforehand, what we share with the writer of our text, or what we share with the community of others who read the text with us or over our shoulder. Midrash is an awareness of greater wholes which empower lesser parts to signify. In this way, it belongs to that area of 'subsidiary knowledge' which Michael Polanyi distinguishes from 'focal knowledge'. Polanyi observes that

> *particulars can be noticed in two different ways.* We can be aware of them uncomprehendingly, i.e. in themselves, or understandingly, in their participation in a comprehensive entity. . . . In the first case we are aware of the particulars *focally*; in the second we notice them *subsidiarily in terms of their participation in a whole.*[1]

I cite Polanyi only to mark that there are points of intersection between midrash and other phenomenological traditions of observation, some of which lie nearer home. But perceiving the participation of a text in a pattern larger than that text is certainly part of the trick. Frank Kermode perhaps expresses it most clearly:

> My purpose has been to suggest that the plain sense of things is always dependent on the understanding of larger wholes and on changing custom and authority. So it must change; it is never naked, but, as the poet says, it always wears some fictive covering. Time itself changes it, however much authority may resist. It must, of course, do so. And it cannot do so if it fails to preserve its foundation text; and short of keeping that text out of unauthorized hands, it cannot prevent readers from making their imaginative additions to the icy diagram. (p. 191)

The status of the 'foundation text' is now seen to be fundamental to midrash and hence to all midrashic interpretation. Midrash cannot operate at all without something to operate on, and that something must be a text, series of texts, commentaries, or even collections of previous midrash, such that something comprehensible can be said about it at all. But, if one is prepared to accept the pre-eminence of some 'foundation text', and prepared to take its presence and its meaning seriously, then it, in its turn, allows of a whole new interpretative freedom which is unavailable to those who work doggedly and determinedly outside the magic circle.

Geoffrey Hartman's own contribution to the book is itself a midrash on an earlier text of his own. It was with the fifth chapter, 'Words and Wounds', of *Saving the Text* that Hartman began the Heideggerian 'turn' back into a concern for words as powerful instruments of human communication. Within this chapter, the section called 'Curse and Blessing' begins with a quotation from Genesis 32: 26–7: 'I will not let thee go, except thou bless me, And he said unto him, 'What is thy name?' The enigmatic struggle at Peniel between Jacob and the man, later to be renamed respectively Israel and God, is the starting point for Hartman's meditation on midrash, and it is the activity of naming itself, of ascribing meaning or divinity to things, that fascinates Hartman as he moves through precursor meditations on Genesis 32.

Midrash and Literature must embody some kind of Pascalian *pari* that interpretation, at this point of its career, needs some kind of return to a 'founding text' if it is not to perish in the desert of its own self-sufficiency. This seems to be clearly implied in Geoffrey Hartman's opening questions:

> The question I have put to myself is: how is this text, the Hebrew Bible, different from all other texts? Is there a basis to the distinction between fiction and scripture? Can we discriminate the two kinds by rhetorical or textual qualities, rather than by external criteria that remain mysterious?

It is a return to logocentrism of the most daring and unrepentant kind, but a whole new interpretative era, drawing upon the newly discovered resources of midrash, is suddenly made possible. May there yet be life after deconstruction?

University of Nottingham

NOTE

1 Michael Polanyi, *Knowing and Being* (University of Chicago Press, Chicago, 1969), p. 128.

PETER HULME

Race

- David Dabydeen (ed.), *The Black Presence in English Literature* (Manchester: Manchester University Press, 1985), 214 pp., £21.50 and £5.95
- David Dabydeen, *Hogarth's Blacks: Images of Blacks in Eighteenth Century English Art* (Mundelstrup: Dangaroo Press, 1985), 155 pp., £6.95
- Henry Louis Gates, Jr (ed.), '"Race", Writing and difference', *Critical Inquiry* (Chicago: University of Chicago), volume 12, number 1 (Autumn 1985).[1]
- Sander L. Gilman, *Difference and Pathology: Stereotypes of Sexuality, Race, and Madness* (Ithaca, NY, and London: Cornell University Press, 1985), 304 pp., $38.45 and $14.25.

In 1973 a member of the House of Lords was heard to describe the differences between Irish Protestants and Catholics in terms of their 'distinct and clearly definable differences of race'. When asked if he could tell them apart, he replied, 'Of course. Any Englishman can.'

These four books are all concerned in their various ways to chart and analyse the signal importance given to 'race' as a trope of irreducible difference, colour being the most obvious instance of that visual sign which is always desired (as by the peer in Henry Louis Gates's anecdote) to make clear and distinct what are felt but often (to lesser mortals) unmarked differences of culture or ideology. *The Black Presence in English Literature* sets out, as its title suggests, with the aim of 'making the black man visible', restoring to our reading of literary texts, and ultimately to the education system, those questions of otherness closed off in the early part of this century by Eliot's construction of a canon of Literature that responded to a supposedly universal human condition. In similar vein, Dabydeen's own book studies the numerous, but previously unregistered, black figures in Hogarth's paintings and engravings, arguing that the blacks, although often seemingly 'marginal', in fact offer a key to unlocking Hogarth's narrative puzzles. Many of the essays in the ' "Race", writing, and difference' collection cover the same kind of ground, though they tend, as *their* title suggests, to deploy the insights, if not of Derrida himself – who does, however, contribute a brief essay on apartheid – then at least of that broadly post-structuralist or new-theoretical criticism which has been, especially in its major practitioners, so resolutely Eurocentric. To put it another way, they tend to be more open towards those larger questions of philosophical 'difference' and psychoanalytical 'otherness' addressed in some of the case studies that make up Sander Gilman's *Difference and Pathology*, where the study of stereotypes is rooted in the universalism of object-relations theory, stereotypes being seen as creations of that universal need to cope with the anxieties engendered by our inability to control our world.

The concept of 'the stereotype', originally and appropriately a late eighteenth-century printing term, is in fact crucial to all these studies of 'othering'. One might imagine that literary and art-historical criticism, with its accumulated expertise about character and type, would have been of assistance here but, as David Dabydeen points out in his study of Hogarth, it is perfectly possible – indeed, the critical norm – for a massively detailed and scholarly examination of, say, *Marriage à la Mode* to expound upon the semantic significance of the cobwebs on the window in one scene, while making no mention whatsoever of the black man serving chocolate right in the centre of another.

After a contextualizing chapter on blacks in eighteenth-century English art and society, and a section on the notion of blackness in philosophical and aesthetic theory, including Hogarth's own *Analysis of Beauty*, Dabydeen moves through Hogarth's major sequences, demonstrating not just the presence of innumerable black figures but their essential importance for a full understanding of Hogarth's complex commentaries on eighteenth-century 'civilization'. Dabydeen's book is in the best tradition of historical scholarship, since it is sharpened by its awareness of questions of colour into new and, by implication, fuller, more 'complete' readings. It also belongs – by general approach and tone rather than explicit affiliation – to the kind of Lukácsian radicalism which wants to enlist the best of the bourgeois tradition. Dabydeen has some difficulty here because he has to recognize the presence of racial stereotypes in Hogarth – for example, the wide-eyed piccaninny in *The Beggar's Opera* – at the same time as arguing that Hogarth is distancing himself from those stereotypes by using them as part of his social critique. In literature the same difficulty is familiar in discussions of Othello and Caliban and Shylock which want to save the Shakespearian appearances by recognizing – or constructing – a distantiated deployment of racist imagery. However, Dabydeen's analyses are often subtle and informed, focusing with equal assurance on the telling detail – for example, the way in which the tobacco pipe functions for Hogarth as an emblem of colonial interests, or the dual meaning of the term 'patron' as 'owner of slaves' or 'supporter of the arts' – and on the larger, imagistic patterns of primitivism and exploitation that articulate the savage commentaries of *A Rake's Progress* and *Marriage à la Mode*. His decisive intervention should make the black presence in Hogarth that bit more difficult to ignore.

In the collection of essays edited by Dabydeen 'making the black presence visible' takes essentially the same critical form. Inevitably figures like Kipling, Forster, Conrad and Buchan feature prominently, if for the most part rather predictably, as 'the literature of Empire' with its range of native 'others'. Ian Duffield's work on Afro-blacks in colonial Australia stands out for its originality, and Abena Busia makes good use of Wilbur Smith's *The Dark of the Sun* (1968) to demonstrate the continued presence of the seminal nineteenth-century figure of the 'buccaneer-hero' in contemporary works of colonialist fiction.

Gates's collection ranges slightly more widely. Anthony Appiah reassesses Du Bois's use of the concept of 'race'; Israel Burshatin has an interesting discussion of the figure of the 'ideal Moor' in fifteenth-century Spanish literature; Patrick Brantlinger offers an extended historical gloss on Marlow's 'place of darkness'; Gayatri Spivak makes visible the blackness of Bertha Mason through a brilliantly attentive reading of Jean Rhys's *Wide Sargasso Sea*; Barbara Johnson rereads with an appropriate degree of self-consciousness the ambiguous work of the black novelist and anthropologist Zora Neale Hurston.

Johnson and Spivak's contributions serve to mark out what can be thought of as the theoretical middle ground occupied by many of the critics writing in these books. Johnson's essay, modest and almost self-effacing, quite different from the pyrotechnics of some of her earlier work, indicates some of the pressures 'a white deconstructor' (her own term) must face when addressing material that cannot be dissipated into mere textual play. Yet Spivak will rightly have nothing to do with what she refers to as the self-conscious rectitude of the 'non-theoretical' approach to Third World literature. In this respect, it is difficult to underestimate the recent influence of Edward Said's *Orientalism* (1978), whose superb deployment of historical scholarship within a broadly Foucauldian framework, alive to the powerful ways in which discourse can construct 'reality', has established 'Foucault' as the sign under which much of the succeeding work in this field has been undertaken. After Said, 'Foucault' can be seen to act as a kind of guarantor of the presence and determining force of 'history, power, knowledge, and society' on questions of textuality, in the face of an insistence, associated with the name of 'Derrida', that 'il n'y a pas d'hors-texte'.[2] It may not be quite clear how we ought to talk about the cultures and societies previously constructed in the West under the general rubric of 'the Orient', but in Said's work at least those 'realities' are never in danger of becoming *simply* textual, a fate whose political consequences could not be contemplated with equanimity. There are questions to be asked about the accuracy of Said's 'Foucault', and about the residual humanism with which potentially awkward questions tend to be diverted, but these are only footnotes to Said's incomparable ability to attend closely and intelligently to the textual construction of events – as he does here in his essay in the Gates collection – at the same time as leaving no doubt about the brute realities of Sabra and Chatila. To put it another way, History, exiled by Structuralism, has returned to the forefront of this area of radical work, where it rejoins – somewhat uneasily at times – the unreconstructed historicism which has never even stopped to ask itself the difficult questions posed by post-structuralism.

Gayatri Spivak ends her essay by suggesting – in a telling image – that the epistemic fracture of imperialism must be reopened by a return to the archives of imperial governance, finding in *Wide Sargasso Sea* the possibility of reading *Jane Eyre* as the orchestration and staging of the self-immolation of Bertha Mason as 'good wife'. The implications of such a possibility can only be developed through a knowledge of the history of the legal manipulation of suttee in British India. The point is well taken, provided, of course, that 'the archives' are not fetishized as the source of an unproblematic 'truth' about imperial policy. Spivak's prompting is answered in at least two essays in the Gates collection. Homi Bhabha works with the *Missionary Register* – a true archive of imperial governance – but takes from it that scene of 'the discovery of the English book', a trope found also in later texts (Conrad, Naipaul), and whose deep ambivalence requires an analysis that will use Foucault but also Freud to plumb its construction of colonial authority. In a slightly different vein, Mary Louise Pratt looks at the 'discourse of manners and customs' which served, eventually under the rubric of ethnography, to mediate the shock of the imperial frontier to the British reading public. Livingstone, Speke, Mungo Park and the rest provide, if not exactly the archives of imperial governance, an important semi-official, and often neglected set of colonial materials. Pratt offers some initial mapping of this territory, highlighting some of its essential types and strategies: the stereotypical portrait of 'the natives', the effacement of the experiencing self, the occlusion of the native bearers, the 'typical day'. Pratt is one of the surprisingly few writers here who show awareness of the recent anthropological work on 'otherness', which is especially valuable – as in Johannes Fabian's *Time and the Other* (1983) – when it forms part of a trenchant re-examination of that discipline's intellectual bases.

Many of the writers here, whether through personal experience or political decision or both, operate within a broadly defined radicalism, anti-racist and anti-imperialist in intent. *Orientalism* again offered an important example, with its commitment at one and the same time to historical scholarship and to a rejection of the supposed neutrality of such scholarship. That issue is never openly rejoined here, though the tension is sensed in the distance between Said's essay, a passionate and compelling denunciation of the 'special case' pleaded by US scholars for Israeli discrimination against non-Jews, and Bernard Lewis's cool and 'objective' account of a group of virtually unknown Afro-Arabic poets writing in the eighth and ninth centuries AD. Gates, the editor, tactfully – and perhaps with a modicum of irony – separates them with an essay entitled 'The politics of Manichean allegory'; but the 'purity' of Lewis's scholarship still stands out oddly in these surroundings. There is no indication of what he is doing writing this piece, what kind of interest or implication the presence of such a group of poets might have, what we might learn today from their poetic inscription of their ethnicity within a classical tradition. With Said – and most of the others here – you know exactly where they stand and why they are writing. Gates, for example, refers to South Africa and the Lebanon as evidence for the continued power in the real world of the concepts that are so easily deconstructed in the small gesture of a scholarly volume. Dabydeen, more locally but just as urgently, explains the significance of the 'Black Presence' conference in Wolverhampton, for so long the platform for Enoch Powell's racist speeches and in 1982 the location of a dispute between a local headmaster and the Sikh community over the right of Sikh children to wear turbans to school. In this context, Lewis's absence of self-explanation and self-situation sounds a false and strangely sinister note: a scholarship that carries no *señas de identidad*, that has nothing to declare, that is not prepared to say where it is coming from, nor where it is headed.

Sander Gilman derives his notion of stereotyping from psychoanalysis, and his brief opening remarks sketch a universal situation of 'good' and 'bad', 'us' and 'them', in which politics also plays no part. In practice, however, his studies of how 'a multitude of historical and social strands lend a given stereotype its particular form' concentrate on the period of the great European colonial empires of the nineteenth century, thereby casting light on many of the facets of colonial discourse, especially in its interconnections with the discourses of sexology and psychology. Typical chapter titles are 'On the nexus of blackness and madness', 'The Hottentot and the prostitute: toward an iconography of female sexuality' and 'Male stereotypes of female sexuality in fin-de-siècle Vienna' (this essay also appears in the Gates volume). Indeed, as this last title might hint, the book can be read as a series of contextualizations for Freud's invention of psychoanalysis.

Contextualization is Gilman's own description of his technique. Typically he will start from a puzzle – say, Freud's extraordinary remark in the *Three Essays on the Theory of Sexuality*, in which he links childhood sexuality, polymorphous perversity and prostitution – and attempt to 'frame a context' in which the remark becomes more comprehensible; in this instance, by charting the medico-legal background (Krafft-Ebbing, Santlus, Hügel) and illuminating it with reference to contemporary pornography and literature. Wedekind and Schnitzler both feature prominently in the essays, but Gilman's range of literary reference is by no means limited to Germany and Austria. Another essay begins with Amos Oz and moves via Altenberg's extraordinary series of sketches, *Ashantee* (1897), to the ethnopornography of Henry Miller and Lawrence Durrell. Yet another frames the context for Jim's disguise in *The Adventures of Huckleberry Finn* – 'Sick Arab – but harmless when not out of his head' – via such texts as the sixth national census of the United States in 1840, Hartmann von Aue's thirteenth-century version of the Ywain legend, and

St Ambrose's commentary on the *Song of Song*'s 'nigra sum, sed formosa'. The wide learning is worn lightly, and usually illuminates.

The scientistic concept of 'race' depends on the establishment of visual differences, preferably ones that can pass themselves off as 'natural'. Perhaps the most forceful of Gilman's chapters looks at the mutual implication between the stigmata of the nineteenth-century's ultimate stereotype of the primitive, 'the Hottentot', and those of the supposedly rampant sexuality of 'the Prostitute'. The myth of female black lasciviousness has a long history. What interests Gilman is the scientific literature which sought proof of that lasciviousness in the unique structure of the Hottentot female's sexual parts, a 'primitive' sexual appetite signalled externally by 'primitive' genitalia. Between 1810 and 1815 a Hottentot female called Saartje Baartman was exhibited in Europe as 'the Hottentot Venus', her genitalia hidden but her protruding buttocks offering a displaced association of excessive female desire. After Baartman's death and dissection, her sexual parts were presented by Cuvier to the Musée de l'Homme where – extraordinarily – they are still on display. Gilman's chapter opens, in fact, in Paris, looking at Manet's two paintings, *Olympia* (1862–3) and *Nana* (1877). Part of his argument is that the black female servant in *Olympia* connotes a sexuality that in *Nana* is found in the central figure's recognized secondary sexual characteristics – her steatopygia and the so-called 'Darwin's ear', established by Lombroso and others as intrinsic features of 'the Prostitute', who thereby became seen as a survival of 'the primitive', one of the many internal others that racked the body of nineteenth-century European society. Gilman's readings of the paintings do not always convince: Olympia's genitals are hardly 'demurely covered' by that aggressively bridged left hand (Tim Clark's essay would have helped him here[3]); but art history surely needs the kind of informed attention to medical and anthropological illustration that Gilman and Dabydeen both provide.

Particularly welcome is Gilman's ability to highlight the nexus of sexual and racial stereotyping through an unmystificatory deployment of psychoanalytical concepts and vocabulary. The understanding of that process of 'othering' by which European discourse constituted its sense of the innate superiority of the healthy white male body is of necessity an interdisciplinary task – as these four books variously and admirably demonstrate. The brute realities of colonial and imperial control must never be forgotten. But colonial discourse – that web of textual practices through which Europe, and later the United States, negotiated and continues to negotiate its relationship with the non-European world and, indeed, with its own 'hyphenated' citizens – can in the end only be understood as psychotic. The reason for this is evident in a number of questions raised, if never satisfactorily answered, in these books.

Why, David Dabydeen never quite asks, should art historians have been so pervasively colour-blind when looking at Hogarth? Why, Edward Said never quite asks, should Israel's Western supporters have allowed their undoubted knowledge of what Israeli policy means for non-Jews to have coexisted so casually with their resolutely positive views of Israeli society? Said goes so far as to see such a syndrome as a symptom of Oedipal blindness, but the reference seems only to connote the tragedy of the situation rather than suggest a potential analysis. After all, Freud does not feature at all in *Orientalism*. 'Blindness' is not a matter of not 'seeing' in some physical sense, but rather a crucial lack of discursive acknowledgement. The English colonists in Virginia could 'see' the native inhabitants growing corn, could draw pictures of that corn, and could write about receiving gifts of corn, but even when starving they would burn cornfields rather than pick the corn, in order to 'prove' to themselves their 'superiority' and enable themselves to write elsewhere about the natives 'roaming' rather than properly settling the land.[4]

Abdul JanMohamed (in the Gates volume) takes issue with Homi Bhabha's attention to the problematics of 'ambivalence' within the discourse of colonial authority. JanMohamed wants to insist on the priority of the political level, but the separation that he himself thereby operates – later using Lacan's 'imaginary' and 'symbolic' for a crude categorization of types of colonialist fiction – merely perpetuates conventional disciplinary distinctions, instead of attempting to build, as Bhabha does, on that essential coupling of the psychoanalytical and the political for an analysis of colonialism. The process of 'othering' which has done much to form the political agenda of the modern world can be understood only if we can speak at the same time of Prospero's power and Prospero's anxiety. Which is why the exemplary work of Frantz Fanon, written over thirty years ago, still has so much to teach us.[5]

University of Essex

NOTES

1 A slightly extended version of this number of *Critical Inquiry* was published in book form by the University of Chicago Press in November 1986.

2 The quotations are from Edward Said, 'The problem of textuality: two exemplary positions', *Critical Inquiry*, 4 (1978), p. 673.

3 T. J. Clark, 'Preliminaries to a possible treatment of *Olympia* in 1865', *Screen*, 21, 1 (1980); developed in chapter 2 of his *The Painting of Modern Life: Paris in the Art of Manet and his Followers* (London: Thames & Hudson, 1985).

4 See Edmund Morgan, *American Slavery, American Freedom: The Ordeal of Colonial Virginia* (New York: Norton, 1975), p. 90; and Francis Jennings, *The Invasion of America: Indians, Colonialism, and the Cant of Conquest* (Chapel Hill, University of N. Carolina Press, 1976), p. 80.

5 Frantz Fanon, *Black Skin, White Masks* (1952), trans. Charles Lam Markmann (New York:, 1967). A new edition, with an introduction by Homi Bhabha, will shortly be published by Pluto Press.

ALAN DURANT

Stylistics

- Roger Fowler, *Linguistic Criticism* (Oxford: Opus
  Books/Oxford University Press, 1986), 190 pp.,
  £4.95

How is it possible, you might want to know, to take seriously a new, introductory work on 'linguistic criticism', after two decades of post-structuralist and deconstructionist critique? Hasn't Stanley Fish, among others, shown that the aspiration of stylistics towards scientificity and timeless formalism is flawed by arbitrariness of judgement and circularity of argument? And hasn't Jacques Derrida shown that, since meaning continually slips away from us as we speak or write, confidence in matters of interpretation – even the aspiration to confidence – is merely flight from the true, radically arbitrary condition of language?

Roger Fowler's *Linguistic Criticism* is exactly a new, introductory work on stylistics propelled into this difficult critical conjuncture. In many ways, the book is simply a solid, traditional guide to the use of linguistics in analysing literary works. But it is also an innovative study, in three interesting and interlocking ways. First, it demonstrates the value of a well-integrated pragmatic dimension in stylistic analysis, relating linguistic forms to interactional and contextual factors, including background assumptions which in practice largely guide interpretation. (It was largely the variability of such background assumptions which undercut the older, textually deterministic aspiration of stylistics towards dispassionate, 'objective' interpretation.) Second, *Linguistic Criticism* – in this respect like much of Roger Fowler's recent work – investigates the consensual, intersubjective nature of interpretation, relating the background of normative values to ideology and social semiotic. This is done by developing a weak version of the Sapir–Whorf hypothesis, while not becoming committed to stronger forms. Partly by developing the Hallidayan idea of the simultaneous existence, within a language, of many different ways of dividing up reality which are articulated in very many different social discourses or 'registers', Roger Fowler avoids the need to take a position on whether or not there are discrete objects in the world independent of linguistic categories. In this respect, his position is not fundamentally dissimilar from that taken in arguments over social knowledge by Barry Hindess and Paul Hirst, or arguably by Michel

Foucault or Hayden White. Third, the book takes up the question of *changes* in systems of background knowledge which surround interpretation. This effectively historicizes the analytic process, and connects the study of linguistic style in a systematic way with broader considerations of social structure, history and the development of ideas.

Together, these three concerns define an innovative stylistic project. It is then the purpose of this new kind of study to free us from patterns of perception and knowledge which are 'habitualized', or sedimented in language during processes of socialization: this would make us resistant to ideological currencies and stale patterns of thought. Simultaneously, study of this kind is intended to sensitize readers to personal habits of perception and usage, linking stylistic criticism back – as, of course, was characteristic of the study of classical rhetoric – with composition and creative activity.

These concerns, of course, fit in not only with much in the thinking of Halliday, and of Sapir and Whorf, but also with much in structuralism and post-structuralism, especially the concern for 'demythologization'. But clearly the aims and techniques of this kind of general discourse analysis are equally well served by examining texts of *any* kind, not just literary works. Indeed, Fowler repeatedly rejects the distinction between 'literary' and 'non-literary' discourse, urging that in education special attention should be given to two non-literary modes of social discourse: 'public, official language', including news, newspapers, contracts, government statements; and 'personal discourse', such as talk between individuals. On what basis, then, given that virtually all extracts considered in the book are from standard literary works, does literature have a special place in all this?

In the Preface to *Linguistic Criticism*, Fowler says the 'chief emphasis' of the book will be on literary examples, though 'I have tried to make it clear that all texts merit this sort of analysis, and that belief in an exclusive category of "literature" or "literary language" is liable to prove a hindrance rather than a help.' Nevertheless, special arguments *are* made in the book for distinguishing literature and non-literature, and these imply a justification for the special focus on literary works as traditionally defined, even while the argument as a whole discredits any such idea.

Centrally, Fowler's argument turns on two terms, 'habitualization' and 'defamiliarization'. 'Habitualization', he argues, has a firm base in cognition: roughly, it means that with familiarity our perceptions become more and more automatic and unanalytic, and that as a result we tend to think within the boundaries of culturally well-established categories. This may help us to build up complex synthetic notions, by allowing us to take basic terms and perceptions for granted; but it has the disadvantage of limiting our ability to have radically new ideas. 'Defamiliarization' is a term adopted from the work of the Russian formalists: literature and other art forms take systems of habitualized communication and make them appear strange, allowing us to see and to rethink things that we have been taking simply in their habitualized forms. But Fowler's idea of 'defamiliarization' differs from most current views of the concept in two major respects. First, Fowler's linguistically functionalist perspective posits links at all levels between formal arrangements in language and structures of social experience and perception; 'defamiliarization', therefore, has to be seen from the outset not as a device that foregrounds particularities of the linguistic code alone, but rather as a process that directly dislodges and reconstructs all our ways of putting together perceptions and ideas. Second, Fowler stresses the historical dimension of habitualization and defamiliarization: through time, he argues, the strange becomes habitual, and is displaced in turn by the strange. This requires that our study of defamiliarization should be historical, if we are to account for the continual supersession and replacement of styles in literature, and in our ways of thinking about the world (p. 37).

Linguistic Criticism is a short, readable and informative guide. It offers a clear account of linguistic approaches to literature, and contains much exemplary exposition of basic linguistic concepts. This readability itself, however, might be thought to work against the book in one way: *Linguistic Criticism* is not clearly organized as a reference book (in the way in which, say, Geoffrey Leech's long-famous *A Linguistic Guide to Poetry* is); and, as a textbook, *Linguistic Criticism* focuses more on arguments for the method and on specific readings than on devices or models for developing skills. This makes the book helpful more as preliminary reading for an academic course than as a textbook for continuous use.

Since linguistic criticism of literature takes place almost exclusively in educational institutions, this question of teaching is a pertinent one. Yet it is only in the last few pages that Roger Fowler discusses pedagogic applications directly. In these pages, he argues that, for his approach to literary study, seminars are more appropriate than lectures or tutorials, and that setting stylistic tasks is attractive because it invites students to do something practical and achievable. I am completely in sympathy with both of these suggestions. But what blunts the edge of *Linguistic Criticism* here is that quite a lot of work has recently been done – in Britain, for example, by Henry Widdowson, Ron Carter, Mick Short and others – in the emerging field of 'pedagogic stylistics'; and consideration of some of this work – for example, its discussion of sequencing of tasks, of problem-solving and general methodology – could have considerably enriched the few observations in this area that Fowler does make.

But is there any useful role for *Linguistic Criticism*, and other work based on describing and interpreting texts from a linguistic viewpoint, given the critiques of stylistics from modern literary theory? My own answer to this question remains yes. What seems possible now – and what may overcome many of the traditional problems of stylistics – is a convergence between the close attention in much contemporary literary theory to the activity of reading (e.g. reader-response criticism) and forms of stylistics which are sensitive to social and historical dimensions of meaning.

Jonathan Culler's idea of 'literary competence' remains perhaps the most established model of reading literature developed in recent years. But what damaged it was its neglect of the socializing processes through which conventional responses to kinds of discourse are established. For literature, as Culler acknowledges, these are familiarity with literary traditions, and education in forms of conventional 'literary' interpretation. Instead of exploring the implications of this, however, Culler chose to emphasize the static, individual possession of 'competence'. In doing so, he seemed to be 'cognitive' at the expense of being 'social' (as Fowler himself argues on p. 176). Since then, counterbalancing emphasis has been given, valuably, to varied readerships and to the active process of *making* readings – especially to such notions as 'interpretive communities', or groups likely to respond to works or kinds of discourse in a similar way. Nevertheless, the separation of 'social' and 'cognitive' remains a damaging simplification. What being a *bearer* of socially constructed ideas or ideology must mean, for example, is that we carry ideas in our minds, to be activated and put to work in any instance in rule-governed inferential procedures. Reading is both a cognitive and a social activity.

What stylistics needs now is further attention to the study of inferential interpretation, with particular regard to two questions. How are inferences triggered by particular linguistic forms (an established issue in pragmatics)? How are socially originated assumptions stored and ranked in memory, and then selected in acts of interpretation (the cognitive issue for a theory of ideology)? This project is not quite as fanciful as it sounds. The development of a new kind of stylistics – and, arguably, of a new approach to ideology – now seems possible, following recent developments in pragmatics and cognitive psychology (perhaps especially Sperber and Wilson's formulation of the theory of relevance). New models of interpretation on these lines would seek to anchor the otherwise utopian 'affective stylistics' Stanley Fish used to prescribe as the remedy for traditional stylistic problems in a more precise account of interpretative inference, thus enabling work in the sociology of reception to be harnessed to issues of reading now. *Linguistic Criticism* is certainly not a study in this new idiom; but in a number of respects it points forward in that direction.

University of Strathclyde

J. M. BERNSTEIN

Unknowing

- Irene E. Harvey, *Derrida and the Economy of Différance* (Bloomington: Indiana University Press, 1986), 285 pp., $24.95
- Christopher Norris, *Contest of Faculties* (London: Methuen, 1985), 256 pp., £16.00 and £6.95

At a certain moment, let us say at the beginning of chapter 6 of Hegel's *Phenomenology of Spirit*, philosophy stopped talking in terms of reason, the transcendental ego, apperception, certainty, monads, noumenon, and all the rest of the technical vocabulary it had gathered together, and suddenly began to talk about a fictional woman whose fate we were instructed to regard as defining both the destiny of Greek civilization as a whole and the working of fate itself as it would pattern succeeding history. Perhaps, although the matter is far from being decided, philosophy managed to master the discourses of history and literature which had so precipitately erupted in its midst in that fateful text. But from that moment on the meaning of philosophy's mastery of its Others was on the agenda; more, the question of philosophy became increasingly the question of its mastery, its domination of and/or submersion in its Others: philosophy and history, philosophy and literature, master and slave, identity and difference.

As Irene Harvey correctly notes, for Derrida Hegel is on the border between the end of metaphysics (philosophy) and the beginning of something else (p. 106); yet, since this description – of a writing that is on the border or, as Derrida has it, 'at the limit of philosophic discourse' – is one which could equally well apply to Derrida's own programme, Derrida's placement (mastering?) of Hegel has something of an uncanny feel about it. It is this uncanniness, however, which is the real strength of Derrida, and the failures and successes of deconstruction relate directly to his ability and inability to sustain this uncanniness in his relations with his two most prominent and dangerously liminal predecessors, Hegel and Heidegger (whose 'history of being' and destruction of Western metaphysics is also a writing at the limit).

Irene Harvey's *Derrida and the Economy of Différance* is the first full-scale philosophic reading of Derrida to appear in English. It opens with a thumbnail comparison of Derrida and Kant – it was Kant, after all, who performed the first, modern, non-sceptical critique of metaphysics – and continues on, in the best chapter of the book, systematically to survey the fundamental gestures of deconstruction as they appear in Derrida's analyses of Husserl and Saussure. Harvey's survey reveals how the 'rigour' of Derrida's writing is metaphysical/philosophical in character, drawing on the conceptual resources of the tradition of metaphysics – necessity, contradiction, and so on – for his subversions of it. This parasitical relation of deconstruction to metaphysics has two consequences, according to Harvey: (1) while not condemned to or redeemable by metaphysics, deconstruction is not detachable from metaphysics either; (2) because this is so, because deconstruction 'inhabits' the texts of the tradition, marking *both* their complicity and non-complicity with metaphysics from *within*, then Derridian deconstructions are *not* critiques. There is, that is to say, no such thing as Derrida's *critique* of Husserl or Saussure or Plato or Heidegger or Hegel, etc. Critique presupposes decidability; the theory in question is either true or false. Derrida's procedure of first inverting hierarchically ordered metaphysical oppositions – above all, presence and absence, identity and difference, speech and writing – and then denying their oppositional character by revealing their origin in a non-originary, necessarily unnameable and therefore 'nicknamed' third (*différance*, trace, supplementarity, writing, *arche*-writing), produces undecidability by producing these undecidables. Undecidability reveals a text's non-identity with *itself*; but, because non-identical with itself, because 'it' 'is' not itself, because the text is not closed in upon or present to itself, then there 'is' no *it* to critique. Deconstructive readings mark texts, leaving tracks in them, but do not overcome, falsify or critique metaphysics. Critique belongs to metaphysics; deconstruction is, Derrida says, the deconstruction of critical dogmatics.

Harvey rightly, clearly and pointedly says all this; but her reading of Derrida cannot quite maintain this perspective, for what she offers in her book is a neo-Schellingian account of Derrida; an account which I have often heard, but which has not heretofore been worked out in print in such a lucid, systematic and telling manner. By neo-Schellingian I mean a theory which articulates the presuppositions – the necessary (transcendental) conditions of possibility – for any given phenomenon beyond self-consciousness (Schelling's move), beyond where the tradition has taken such enquiry to a point or moment of 'indifference' which lies 'outside' the oppositional terms of metaphysics, and which cannot be either empirically named or reflectively comprehended. Now, on the neo-Schellingian approach, 'that which is overturned is ultimately sustained but nonetheless situated in a "wider", more all-encompassing context wherein the limits of the former become explicit' (p. 77); and this does sound very much like Hegelian *Aufhebung*, the metaphysical gesture *par excellence* for Derrida. While Harvey attempts to mitigate the Hegelian overtones and resonances of the move to a more all-encompassing third, the whole thrust of her reading says otherwise.

According to what might be called the standard deconstructive analysis,

Derrida *uses* the transcendental form of argument against itself, so that the moment of indifference, of *différance,* trace, and so on, does *not* reveal a wider context but rather the 'bottoming out' of the metaphysical assumptions which make transcendental argument an intelligible, rational form of argumentation. Hence, on the standard deconstructive reading, undecidables reveal the always transgressed limits of metaphysics, while on the neo-Schellingian reading they represent nonexistent but none the less 'real' conditions for the metaphysical systems ('restricted economies') which, although knowable through their effects, cannot be known or accounted for in traditional metaphysical terms. Their interaction with metaphysics is just the economy of *différance.*

Derrida's programme, I suspect, is closer to the standard deconstructive account than to the neo-Schellingian approach. That Harvey has misread Derrida in a neo-Schellingian way is not, however, just her doing; nor is it, as one might too easily surmise, the exigencies of metaphysics itself working their way out through her reading. Rather, there is a certain tension in Derrida's writings that precipitates a reading like Harvey's as one of its consequences. The tension is easy to spot but difficult to negotiate firmly. Stated broadly, the issue is one of the necessity of deconstruction; stated more narrowly but more perspicuously, the issue is, as Harvey rightly claims (pp. 74–5, 123, 204–5, 212), the repeatability and hence ideality of deconstructive practices. How is the repeatability/ideality and hence necessity of deconstruction to be explained and understood? On the one hand, the answer to this question which satisfies the requirements of the standard deconstructive approach claims that the necessity of deconstruction is strictly historical and conjunctural in character. According to this account, Derrida specifies metaphysics historically, as an epoch, as a non-unified totality itself subject to a certain compulsion to repeat. Practising philosophy at the close of this epoch amounts to reading it as compelling a closure it cannot, can never, establish. Hence the repeatability and ideality of deconstruction is borrowed from the history it haplessly reinscribes. Deconstruction marks our inability either to do metaphysics or to escape it; metaphysics is the nightmare from which we are trying to awake.

On the other hand, one of the metaphysical concepts most in need of deconstruction is 'history', the narrative movement from presence to self-presence (pp. 102–3). The deconstruction of 'history', as the concept which gives deconstruction its epochal character, has the consequence of 'universalizing' the process of deconstruction, of de-limiting, that is, of re-moving the historical limits which would make it unequivocally conjunctural. Once this is accomplished, then the path is open to the induction Harvey proposes:

> Of course *différance* is not a thing and is certainly not to be found within the orbit of what metaphysics calls the 'same'. Nevertheless, have we not uncovered here a certain *concept* of *différance* which transcends specific situations, circumstances, and texts? After all, is it not Derrida himself

who claims that the 'proper name' is not a reliable index for that which we call a 'textual system'? . . . for Derrida, as we know, there is a more fundamental structure (metaphysics itself in this case) which links one context-specific text (Freud) to another (Plato). The proper name is thus an unreliable index for what he calls the *context* of a *text*. It is thus that Derrida is able to trace from one 'text' to another various systems of metaphors which, in relation to the structures of metaphysics, profoundly link them together into one tradition. (p. 212)

And in the penultimate paragraph of her book Harvey concludes: 'Perhaps it is thus that *différance* has no proper name and exceeds all conceptualizing as such, yet can it therein exceed all transcendental formulation of the same? We have suggested that it cannot.'

Against Harvey it might be urged that the deconstruction of the concept of history does not entail its disappearance or undermine Derrida's dependence on it for the understanding of the necessity of his programme, any more than the deconstruction of any other concept can eliminate or ultimately displace it. Further, Derrida's nicknaming, naming according to circumstances, of his non-concepts certainly reveals his intention to block, or at least not be caught up in the kind of inductive argument which Harvey performs. And while, in the final analysis, nothing can certainly prohibit the formation of a concept from a practice – something that Derrida would be the first to admit – the possibility, perhaps even the inevitability of so doing does not make the gesture of formation 'right' or 'illuminating'. Finally, following Harvey makes problematic what exactly the *point* of deconstruction might be: how does her economy of *différance* help avoid the violence of metaphysics, its endless strategic mastery? What makes being placed in the wider context of the economy of *différance* a happier, better, less dominated place to be?

With Harvey, however, one cannot but note that, first, Derrida appears to affirm transcendental enquiry more unambiguously than suggested above.[1] Second, unlike Merleau-Ponty and others, who attempt to criticize Husserl on the basis of a denial of his distinction between 'essence' and 'fact', Derrida's analysis of Husserl focuses on his equation of absolute being with a phenomenologically purified self-consciousness, thus firmly echoing Schelling's critique of Fichte.[2] Finally, in reading Derrida one simply does not find the kind of heightened sense of a historical predicament or the historical awareness and specificity that punctuates the texts of Hegel and Heidegger.

Because she so tenaciously follows through the neo-Schellingian elements in Derrida's thought, Harvey's work correctly questions the easy critical appropriation of Derrida, and forces us thus to consider the historical pertinence of the project of deconstruction.

Another way of stating the previous point might be this. Part of the power and appeal of deconstruction, and hence some of the reason for its considerable cultural impact, derives from its critical capacity to undo and undermine a wide variety of apparently stable conceptual views and operations. And, indeed, Derrida states, 'deconstruction is not neutral. It intervenes.' To be sure; but in the name of what and from where? Because Derrida does not engage in critique as such, and because the nature of deconstruction involves assigning a 'certain legitimacy' (p. 81) to the system deconstructed, a kind of historical and critical levelling, a neutrality to the second degree, comes to inhabit deconstruction. Using Harvey's terms of reference for the moment, in deconstruction different metaphysical systems come to be relativized to the wider context of the economy of *différance*; this operation, while unsettling and intervening in *each* system, none the less engenders a parity, a neutrality of these various systems with respect to one another which the specifics of Derrida's readings cannot itself overcome. But are all these systems really equally worthy of our attention, equally insightful (knowing) and blind (unknowing) on the questions they discuss? Does not reading deconstructively force Derrida to be too respectful to, say, Husserl? Does not deconstruction end up *more* unknowing than the plurality of texts it engages precisely because it leaves all of them in their relations to one another just as it found them? Does not the fact that deconstruction *'ne veut rien dire'* entail an a priori neutrality that undercuts its empirical disruptions?

For Hegel the history of metaphysics is bound up with the coming-to-be and domination of abstract, Kantian reason; for Heidegger the history of being engenders the fatalities of modern technology. In both cases the overcoming of metaphysics was bound up with an analysis of modernity. That analysis was the *position* from which the question of metaphysics was raised, and the overcoming of modernity as analysed was the ultimate point towards which their questioning aimed. Their philosophizing at the limit was their way of thinking the unthinkable: the catastrophes of a finite present which was a form of metaphysics. Is there any comparable 'position' in Derrida? Is not the uncanniness of his deconstructions parasitic on positions that are not his *own*? Can one question anything without taking a position, without being there?

I suspect that we so readily appropriated Derrida as a critical theorist through a kind of intellectual optical illusion: the deconstruction of presence/logocentrism *looked* so like Barthes's (Brecht-inspired) critique of naturalization (as *the* ideological operation) in the name of history that the former naturally appeared as a more philosophical, systematic and rigorous version of the latter. That this was an illusion should be, by now, evident.

Christopher Norris's collection of elegant essays is a perfect reflection of the critical impasse which Harvey's book puts painfully before us. Norris is anxious to sustain the critical thrust of received deconstruction, while being none the less aware of what I have termed its a priori neutrality, or what might be otherwise diagnosed as relativism. In Norris's hands the latter issue is worked through somewhat obliquely, since he tends to displace the problem of the rejection of theoretical mastery on to hermeneutics (Gadamer) and pragmatism (Rorty), and hence fails to engage it in connection with deconstruction proper.

Norris's best essays, those attacking Rorty, Scruton, Fish and Hart, have less to do with deconstruction than with traditional ideological critique, and are none the worse for it. In them Norris confidently and persuasively reveals those moments and strategies where(by) his antagonists dissimulate their value positions into a presumed 'natural' relation between 'history, reason and present-day consensus values' (p. 9). Naturalization is a strategy of ideological legitimation, and both Rorty's critique of meta-narratives and Fish's institutional theory of meaning and interpretation are naturalizing and legitimating in character. There can be little doubt that their resistance to theory, like Scruton's Wittgenstein-inspired resistance, is intended to block radical criticism and perpetuate liberal orthodoxy; it is the 'end of ideology' all over again. What is worth pointing out here, however, is that, while Norris refers to deconstruction in lodging his critiques of these writers, the *force* of his criticisms, in the end, always relies upon the Barthesian axiomatic identification of naturalization with ideological legitimation. Indeed, Norris appears to concede that this is his view of deconstruction quite explicitly: 'Above all, deconstruction holds out to the last against those forms of pre-emptive consensus thinking which substitute a naturalized "narrative" ethos for the work of critical reflection' (p. 42). So, for example, his critique of Rorty ultimately repeats the standard Marxist criticism of the realist novel (pp. 157–8). This is not to question the force of Norris's critiques in any way – indeed, they seem to me in all their essentials correct – but rather to begin to question his placement of deconstruction on the side of the angels and Marxism.

There is too much that needs saying here to say much clearly; so I shall restrict myself to a few points that are directly relevant to Norris's own shot-gun marriage.[3] First on the agenda must be the question of theory itself. In comparison to Rorty's and Fish's pragmatism, and certainly in comparison to those naïve critical practices that believe themselves to be 'theory-free', deconstruction appears theoretical. But, as has been pointed out, deconstruction itself, especially as practised by Derrida, contains a certain resistance to theory, where theory is taken to equal not rational, principled argument, but argument to or from first principles. Norris is quite clear that he opposes the first, pragmatist, sort of resistance to theory, but appears distinctly uneasy when it comes to evaluating deconstruction's own resistance to theory. On the one hand, he wants to follow Habermas's transcendental defence of enlightened reason as a means of sustaining *rational* criticism (a preference that comes through well in his nicely modulated comparison of Empson and de Man in chapter 3); while, on the other hand, he consistently defends de Man's undermining of the autonomy of theory from literature. To say, as Norris appears to say, that Habermas goes a little too far in the direction of pure theory, as Habermas himself now admits, while deconstruction 'has at least the very positive political virtue of opposing itself squarely to the naturalized consensus of "post-modern" liberal reason' (p. 38), is to say too little. What is at issue here is the question of mastery itself: when does the operation of reason (theory) become domination? Is it only when instrumental rationality trespasses into the life-world of intersubjective communication, as Habermas avers, or is the whole Western tradition of reason, which opposes literal truth to fictive (metaphorical) play, an operation of domination, as deconstruction claims?

Let us for the moment, *pace* Norris (I think), assent to the latter contention and its presumption of the necessity and legitimacy of totalizing critique; even here, deconstruction and Marxism would part ways. Adorno – who like the deconstructionists regards the split between truth and fiction, philosophy and literature, as factitious and a source or symptom of domination – diagnoses the realization of enlightened reason, which governs and perpetuates this duality, in terms of capital and its domination of exchange-value (sameness/identity) over use-value (non-identity, difference). It is this diagnosis, and the genealogy of reason lying behind it, which gives point to his negative dialectic. To put the same point otherwise, for Adorno the domination of reason over literature is both caused by and is a sign of economic domination; further, this domination as it becomes manifest on the side of art and literature reveals the irrationality lying at the heart of what we call reason. Derrida, and arguably de Man, arrive at a similar sounding place from another direction. Derrida belongs squarely within the tradition of modernism, where modernism is taken as a movement from presence to self-presence. So modernism in painting is the movement whereby painting comes to have painting, representing and seeing, as its object; literary modernism is the literary questioning of the practice of writing literature. Derrida is a philosophical modernist with a difference; he does not ask the question 'What is thinking?' but rather the literary question 'What is writing?' *in* philosophy.[4] What gives Derrida's line of interrogation its general import and legitimacy is his demonstration of the sign as being the fundamental or pivotal metaphysical operator. What makes the significance of Derrida's project so difficult to assess is that it *begins* with the subversion of the distinction whose institutional effects Adorno's Marxism seeks to unmask as a sign of the operation of capital. If this argument is right, then Norris is correct in aligning deconstruction with reflective overcoming and critique; but it is altogether unclear, as unclear as Marxism's relation to modernism in general, how far this brings deconstruction into accord with Marxism. The reason for this ambiguity is not difficult to locate: what I earlier pointed out as Derrida's lack of an independent analysis of modernity is not a contingent feature of his programme; on the contrary, his unknowing strategy of subversion, his lack of a position, is inscribed in his project from its inception.

This raises a related point, namely the very idea of Marxism finding a *use* for textualist theory. One apparent presupposition of this thesis is that deconstruction can be used because it has no *telos* proper to itself, nor could it, given its standpoint concerning teleology and the proper, not to speak of 'itself'. Even if this is conceded, the problem still arises as to the legitimacy of applying a theory, one of whose central concerns has been to question the subordination of practice to theory. Surely this is at the very centre of the question of theoretical mastery. How can it be legitimate for Marxist theory – whose own theoretical attempt to master history is itself in question – to use textual theory, whose *raison d'être* is the denial of theoretical autonomy, in order to carry out its (Marxism's) critical ends? Norris is not unaware of this difficulty, but rather than engage it he simply concedes and denies it at a stroke:

> Deconstruction is not an antagonist discourse which Marxism must work to discredit by exposing its ideological motives. Neither is it merely a handy appendage that Marxists can adapt – with a little ingenuity – to their own more practical purposes. Rather, it is the currently most advanced form of that critical reflection upon knowledge and interests which remains indispensable to Marxist thought. (pp. 35–6)

That deconstruction, especially in the hands of Derrida and de Man, possesses a radical, critical energy and trajectory it would be pointless to deny. Yet, as the lucid texts of Harvey and Norris demonstrate, appropriating that radicality is not easily managed, since each gesture of appropriation transgresses the transgressive relation between deconstruction and the tradition of metaphysics. Moreover, despite their shared pre-occupations, the works of Derrida and de Man press in different directions. As a brief example: from 'The rhetoric of temporality' to the end of *Allegories of Reading* de Man essayed the possibility that subject and subjectivity (so-called) were *grammatical* substitutions, were grammatical mistakes.[5] Meanwhile, Derrida's *metaphorics* of life, death, phallocentrism, castration, hymen, dissemination, parasite, and so on, provides textual functions and operations with a vitalistic and sexual aura which owes something (but what?) to Nietzsche and Freud, but whose force (what is it?) is quite distinctive. A small example, yet the questions raised by it are large, since it throws into question the *nature* of textuality itself. If texts are not mere texts, if in engaging in textual practices, if in tracing the play of a text, we do not know *what* a text *is*, then caution is advised: we might be playing with fire.

University of Essex

NOTES

1 Jacques Derrida, *Of Grammatology*, trans. Gayatri Spivak (Baltimore, Md: Johns Hopkins University Press, 1967), p. 50.
2 Ibid., p. 50. I owe the point about Husserl to Peter Dews.
3 I can only state here that unlike Norris I find Ryan's treatment of the marriage unconvincing. More promising, perhaps, is some of the recent work of Gayatri

Spivak and Andrew Parker. For examples, see their respective essays in *Diacritics* (Winter 1985).

4 I owe this formulation of Derrida's position to my student Olivier Serafinowicz.

5 On 'The rhetoric of temporality', see my *The Philosophy of the Novel* (Brighton: Harvester Press, 1984), pp. 225–7. On *Allegories of Reading*, see Barbara Johnson, 'Rigorous unreliability', *Yale French Studies*, 69 (1985), pp. 73–80.

NICOLAS TREDELL

Desire

- Norman Bryson, *Tradition and Desire: From David to Delacroix* (Cambridge: Cambridge University Press, 1984), 250 pp., £30

Pliny's *Natural History* tells us that Zeuxis of Heraclea painted grapes so lifelike that birds flew down to eat from the vine. Norman Bryson takes this as the 'central anecdote in Western aesthetics'. It epitomizes the belief that painting's aim is to produce a representation of reality so complete that the materiality of paint, the trace of the painter's labour, the conventions of signifying systems, dissolve into the reality itself. The three narratives of painting's development still dominant in art history – Pliny's, from antiquity; Vasari's *Lives of the Artists*, from the Renaissance; and E. H. Gombrich's *Art and Illusion*, from our own time – all, in their respective ways, present the history of painting as an evolution towards the Essential Copy of universal visual experience. For Pliny and Vasari, the development of painting is inductive; for Gombrich it involves, as in Popper's philosophy of science, a constant testing of the schema, the inherited formula, against reality, a progressive elimination of error.

But these optimistic accounts turn against themselves to imply a darker version, in which tradition threatens the artist with a paralysing sense of belatedness. For example, the relationship of neophyte to precursor in Gombrich is in fact one of antagonism, of a necessary iconoclasm that seeks to miscognize not only the details but the *principles* of the predecessor's work. Bryson finds this suggestive of a more adequate theory of tradition that draws on the ideas of the past as burden and of the 'anxiety of influence' propounded, in literary studies, by W. Jackson Bate and Harold Bloom, and on the implications of the proposition that 'painting is an art of the sign'. Tradition is less benign legacy than potential mortmain; artistic change is not an evolution towards the Essential Copy, but a troping or turning of tradition through the material practice of a desiring and mortal body in and upon signs. Bryson explores this theory in relation to the work of David, Ingres and Delacroix.

We associate David with neo-classicism; and neo-classicism, Bryson contends, is a lethal style. It denies the painter's right to war with tradition at all; it puts him in a double-bind, enjoining both repetition and innovation. The neo-classical painter who would achieve his own identity must secretly turn tradition, while seeming to restore it. *Antiochus and Stratonice*, which won David the 1774 Prix de Rome, employs the trope of aegis. It invokes precursors for protection, as a guarantee of conformity that also serves as a cover for, and a means of, covert subversion: past masters are put into play against each other – in this case, Pietro da Cortona and Poussin. But this trope may trap the painter in mimicry, leaving him no scope for innovation. In *Antiochus and Stratonice*, however, the play of styles is starting to merge into a concern with what Bryson calls 'visuality': the vision of the figures in the painting is split by their insertion into the world of others and signs – for example, Antiochus cannot look with frank desire at Stratonice, his father's wife. This relates to the constraints that David's precursors place upon his visuality as a painter. The concern with visuality is developed in *Belisarius Begging Alms*, which uses the trope of catachresis, wrenched conjunction. The neo-Poussinist, neo-classicist 'severe manner' and the *drame bourgeois* of Greuze, history and genre painting, are yoked together, to fuse and clash. The stylistic splits in the painting are matched in its narrative register, especially in regard to visuality: for instance, the woman who gives alms to Belisarius and the child is split by different images coming to her that seem to demand different self-projections from her – citizen, donor, mother – while Belisarius's blindness disrupts the gendered visual order in which man is the Bearer of the Look.

Bryson's concept of visuality challenges the 'natural' account of vision, long dominant in the West, which holds that impressions of the world enter the eye to be received by a unitary 'I' and excludes the social, interpersonal aspects of vision. In contrast, visuality proposes, not merely an 'I'/eye receiving impressions of the world, but complex negotiations between eye, self, world, others and signs. The continuum of my visual experience is split by the intervention of signifying systems and by my awareness of my visibility, through those systems, to the eyes of others. The split in the field of gender is especially important. From the first, one must shape one's self-image and self-projections to others in male/female terms. This very interesting discussion of visuality leads up to a compelling analysis of David's most astonishing work, *The Oath of the Horatii*:

> The *Oath* is an exact image of visuality for the subject living under patriarchy. The females, denied political authority by the patriarchal mandate, are consigned to silence, to the interior, to reproduction; while simultaneously the males are inserted into the equally destructive registers of language and of power convergent in the oath. . . . The visual space of the males is filled with objects caught in the transfer, from sign to sign, of the patriarch's power. It originates in a body that can no longer sustain the weight of power: the patriarch is now weaker than his sons, his debility stressed by David in the instability of his pose, arms and legs bent where the legs and arms of the sons are straight, the left foot uncertainly placed, while the feet of the sons are square with the ground. From this source the charge moves to the first of its relays, the

swords, to the second, the taut and outstretched arms, and on to invest the bodies of the sons with every mark of virile possession, from the spear, to the stiffly erect crest of their helmets, to the dilated veins of their arms; it energises the oath they swear, re-dedicating the body to the description coming to it from the outside and re-consecrating that description through the flesh.

The visuality of the viewer of the *Oath* is also split, by its use of two contradictory modes of representation – perspective and frieze – and by its fusion of *veduta* with narrative centre. In perspectival painting, the *veduta*, the organization of all lines around a clear, central vanishing point, constructs the viewer as unitary 'I'/eye, visual monarch of what s/he surveys. But this can always turn against the viewer, emphasizing the point he or she cannot occupy, converting him or her into an image, displacing the viewer's mastery. And in the *Oath* the reversible vanishing point is also the narrative centre where the sons' hands take from their father the swords to which they swear their flesh; this collapses the subject position of detachment from represented disorder which neo-classicism seems to offer.

The *Oath* challenges the power of the past over David's visuality as a painter in an apparently paradoxical way: by an apparently rigorous return to it. No *Académie* pussyfooting here: the *Oath* is uncompromisingly antique: and antiquity is thus made strange, no longer the familiar, reassuring source and guarantee of eighteenth-century civilization. The *Oath*, for its first audiences, is a shock, a radical break. Its return to pure antiquity makes it new. It does not, of course, go back to antique *painting*: that has not survived. In this sense the *Oath* constructs and inevitably surpasses its supposed precursors. But it does return to antique *sculpture*: the picture has the hardness of stone, and in this respect functions as an image of tradition itself – a force of petrifaction. Here again, acknowledgement of the power of the past makes for violent innovation. But the *Oath* is a tragic triumph; David paints *'the mortality of sight'*: the fact that each of us must see across the sign systems that precede and will survive us. The relationship between sight, signs, bodies, representations and death was one David was to learn much more about – and to paint, unforgettably, in *Marat assassiné* – in the French Revolution.

David, recanting, survived the Revolution, but as a lessened artist. His greatest pupil, Ingres, is known as the arch-conservative antagonist of Delacroix. But Bryson argues that in fact Ingres's closest kinship is with Delacroix, that in its guise of orthodoxy his work subversively tropes tradition. For example, his *Imperial Portrait of Napoleon* playfully employs the trope of totality, alluding to all the precursors, so that 'the painting is like a speeded up film of Western art from Phidias to Raphael, in ten seconds'. This range and rapidity of reference helps Ingres to elude tradition's weight. The portraits of the Rivière family use the trope of aegis; but the ways in which they invoke the protector, Raphael, and their spatial contradictions, set off a chain of signifying displacements that constantly defer the presence especially expected of portraiture, and open the play of desire. Bryson identifies counter-presence, or desire, as Ingres's most crucial trope, because of its direct link with sexual desire. *Jupiter and Thetis*, for instance, finds the sexual, not *in* bodies, but in their deformation out of presence; this discloses the intervals of desire, the gap between the actual and the sign. Bryson takes issue with John Berger's comparison, in *Ways of Seeing*, between *La Grande Odalisque* and a pin-up; *La Grande Odalisque* is 'radically dehiscent', a two-dimensional design that, when one tries to flesh it out into three dimensions, bursts apart, disrupting the stereotype of woman that the pin-up provides. But Bryson finds Ingres's most complex enactment of the trope of counter-presence in, unexpectedly, the *Vow of Louis XIII* – undoubtedly a conservative affirmation, against Romanticism, of Catholicism, monarchy, nation, family, but also a disclosure of the desire which these institutions both utilize and seek to deny. The discrepancies between the multiple invocations of Raphael in the *Vow*, the fissure between the upper and lower halves of the painting, the unstable design of the Madonna's features that 'implies a suite of *permutations* in which no combination can be final', all work to postpone presence, to open absence and activate desire. This also happens in the Ingres painting that most appeals to the twentieth century, the *Madame Moitessier* portrait; for instance, the high-fidelity rendering of her dress plays against the low-fidelity rendering of her face and arms, and the images in the mirror behind her do not match what they supposedly reflect. *Madame Moitessier* is a 'fissile and disruptive masterpiece' setting off 'a vertigo of displacements that return the viewer to his or her own desire, to the body in dispossession'. Its agon with tradition employs the trope of reversal; it is so much stronger than its sources – a first-century Herculaneum fresco and an unfinished Raphael design worked up by his studio, synecdoches for antiquity and Raphael – that time is nearly turned round, almost making it seem that 'Ingres is being *imitated by his ancestors*'.

Bryson's discussion of Delacroix concentrates on the relatively neglected decorative cycle on the ceiling of the Library of the Chamber of Deputies in the Palais Bourbon: a work difficult of access, and arduous to view. The images in the half-domes at each end of the cycle – *Orpheus Civilizing the Greeks* and *Attila Destroying Italy and the Arts* – offer an apparently clear opposition: Foundation/Holocaust. Each affirms the visual as the sign of civilization: Orpheus has a scroll instead of a lyre; Attila, a figure of blind fury, destroys the visual arts. But the aural associations of Orpheus trouble visual primacy, while the power of the *visual* representation of Attila inevitably seems, in a way, a celebration of his *blind* violence. The subversive connotations of each painting are amplified by their interaction, and by the twenty subordinate paintings, in five domes, that stretch between them. For example, the implied hierarchy in the picture of Archimedes about to be killed by the soldier is undermined by Archimedes' evident neglect of his body and the soldier's physical discipline. The cycle is palindromic: it can be read in both an Orphic-sublimating and an anti-Orphic desublimating direction. Whereas Michelangelo's Sistine Ceiling aims at unequivocal oppositions and the end of desire in the Gaze of God, the meanings of the Bourbon Library cycle have the fluidity, the reversibility, the fragmentariness of the Glance – it is physically impossible for the viewer in the Library to take in the cycle as a whole. The Glance makes mobile sense of the cycle, but not just as it likes: the figure of reversal in the narrative register of the cycle is enacted in the visual, semantic and somatic activity of the viewer; s/he also is always too early or too late. Delacroix's easel painting defers closure by foregrounding the painterly trace; in the Bourbon Library, the trace cannot be seen so high, but the deferment of closure is effected in narrative terms, by the collapse of the comprehensive story that the cycle seems to promise. Culture is not contemplated as product but enacted as process, simultaneously constructive and destructive, in the glance, the body, the desire of the viewer.

The activity of the Bourbon Library cycle, as evoked by Bryson, might serve as an image of his own book. *Tradition and Desire* enacts, provokes its reader to enact, a challenge, not only to the conventional categories of art history, but to all those concepts of culture that seek to petrify. Of course, it raises questions that need pressing further: can mimesis be wholly explained in terms of conformity to culturally relative notions of the real? Are 'absence' and 'desire' in danger of becoming new forms of the transcendent signified? How does painting, as an 'art of the sign', relate to other signifying systems? Does Bryson dissect too much? Would the artists he discusses recognize themselves in his account? But this is, none the less, a resourceful, exciting book.

BRIAN COATES

Feminism

- Toril Moi, *Sexual/Textual Politics: Feminist Literary Theory*, New Accents (London: Methuen, 1985), 224 pp., £9.95 and £4.95
- Elaine Showalter (ed.), *The New Feminist Criticism: Essays on Women, Literature and Theory* (London: Virago, 1986), 416 pp., £11.95 and £5.95
- Gayle Greene and Coppelia Kahn (eds), *Making a Difference: Feminist Literary Criticism*, New Accents (London: Methuen, 1985), 288 pp., £14.95 and £5.95

Woman-in-discourse, the topic of these texts, is situated close to the heart of the post-structuralist project. Feminist literary theory and criticism posits a number of philosophical/metaphorical contextualizations that alert us to the patriarchy of traditional humanism, the 'secret intersections of sexuality and textuality', the inexorably reductive and political nature of all reading practice. These texts indicate the affinity of such thought with recent radical analyses of the Western intellectual tradition. Such issues as whether woman names a being or a position in discourse, how far sexuality can be differentiated from social encoding or is strictly subsequent to socialization, and whether political and aesthetic reading strategies are necessarily conflated through the pressures of ideological forms can be traced through all of the texts.

Toril Moi addresses herself to the theoretical premises of feminist criticism. Her concern with 'the metaphysical nature of gender identities' leads to a questioning of the difference of women except in so far as difference represents a step away from patriarchal oppression. Radical feminism demands an inversion of current gender norms but only in order that such norms can ultimately be deconstructed. Moi associates Kristeva and Derrida with this aim. Masculinity and femininity are yet another binary opposition that seeks to close off experience and thought. Reifying gender terminology falsifies the Kristevan semiotic which lies before (in the pre-Oedipal phase) and beyond (in contradiction, in silence) the centred speaking subject. The complicating issue lies in the interplay of politics and criticism. Asexuality, like New Criticism, is defined here as a neutering conservatism, a smuggled patriarchal value system whose bland transparencies obscure the processes of signification. Annette Kolodny, Elaine Showalter and Myra Jehlen are found by Moi to have remained within 'the lineage of male-centred humanism' because they stress the authoritative nature of feminine texts and feminist readings, retain the notion of the 'integrity' of the text and praise liberal pluralism.

Establishment feminist critics working in academia are subject to the institutional constraints through which jobs, tenure and promotion are channelled. This qualification accounts, in part, for these uneasy dealings with ideology. The elisions in American feminist criticism that lead from a corrective emphasis upon women's experiences in reading and writing to comparativist readings of and by men and women cannot of themselves throw up a non-patriarchal theory of literature. Between Lilian Robinson's credo – 'I am not terribly interested in whether feminist criticism becomes a respectable part of academic criticism; I am very much concerned that feminist critics become a useful part of the women's movement' – and Myra Jehlen's distinction between 'appreciative' and 'political' readings lies space for that convergence of feminism and deconstruction that is a prominent feature of French feminist criticism.

Moi's discussion of Hélène Cixous, Luce Irigaray and Julia Kristeva offers a no-nonsense summary of what she terms the ' "heavy" intellectual profile' of French feminist thought. Again the problematic interaction of 'theory' with patriarchal practice shapes the form of the discourse. Cixous's unpacking of binary thought is aligned with Derrida's promotion of *différance*. Feminism provides a political bite. 'Either woman is passive or she doesn't exist' is how Cixous articulates the oppressive power of patriarchal hierarchies. *Écriture féminine* (a useful term disowned by Cixous, who prefers 'writing said to be feminine') defines a post-binary, 'open' writing, 'to want the two, as well as both' that is (mostly) the prerogative of the biological female. Colette, Duras and Genet apparently espoused this form. Cixous's wavering approach to biologism is seen by Moi as a departure from the deconstructive enterprise, though a loosening of the analysis by attention to Cixous's privileging of key metaphors – Gift/Proper, Castration/Decapitation, Voice/Law, Milk/Honey, Word/Sea, Writing/God, Water–Womb–Ocean, Text, Mother-text, Rape-text, Nipple/Penis – reveals the extraordinary range of this project. To read metaphysical presence into the fragmentary, elusive, polyphonic voicings of Cixous is to undermine the dissolution of coherence, the radical politicization of discourse that is generated by a frustrating of the reader's rage for order.

Luce Irigaray's *Speculum de l'autre femme* makes play with such expectations by basing its shape on the speculum/vagina. We read backwards, Freud to Plato, the two separated by 'speculum', in the innermost cavity of which is Descartes. Moi comments: 'woman constitutes the silent ground on which the patriarchal thinker erects his discursive constructs.' Irigaray's displacement of the canon of Western thought (another Derridian manœuvre) tackles the question of how concepts can be generated without metaphysical presence by contextualizing (as in *Speculum*), by mimicry of male discourse (Margaret Thatcher, Moi's test case, is an astutely selected instance of the way in which political contexts inform the practice of mimicry), and by a theory of women's 'morphology'. The geography of a woman's sex, argues Irigaray, is comprehensive: 'a woman touches herself constantly . . . her sex is composed of two lips which embrace continually.' The sexed metaphorical contrast, 'touch'/'sight', is Irigaray's equivalent of Cixous's the Gift and the Proper.

Julia Kristeva, the final theorist discussed, presents a neo-formalist position within linguistics. Attention to the boundaries of language meaning/making will allow us to recuperate a heterogeneous signifying poetic practice beyond binarism. 'Woman as such does not exist', she is a positioning, marginal, neither inside nor outside, Lilith and Virgin, Whore and Mother of God, on the border.

The two anthologies reviewed here also deal with the relation between feminism and deconstruction and with the theory/praxis issue sparked off by the connection. Greene and Kahn worry that 'deconstruction may lead to a scepticism which is used to justify the evasion of political positions' but confirm that 'a deconstructive feminist criticism is potentially revolutionary'. Nelly Furman's essay on 'The politics of language', considering feminist criticism of the absence of women's experience in literature and of the presence of weak stereotypes, notes that representation can itself be seen as a patriarchal paradigm. Interestingly, she responds to this issue with the same passage from Derrida and MacDonald's 'Choréographies' that closes Moi's book. This passage pleads for a 'multiplicity of sexually marked voices . . . a sexuality without number'. Derrida reads the feminist case as a special instance of the deconstructive cleansing process that all value systems must be subjected to. The discussion of French feminist criticism by Ann Rosalind Jones (like Bonnie Zimmerman, represented in both books) stiffens this view by presenting feminist deconstruction as a deconstruction of criticism. She quotes Josette Féral as wishing to 'interrogate that discourse about its own conditions of production'. Jones manages in these essays to draw out the subversive and revolutionary nature of French feminist thought in a way that sharply differentiates it from the solid (and no doubt necessary) reworking of patriarchal canon formation and image stock that is the main work of the Anglo-American critics in these texts.

While Lilian Robinson does not wish feminist criticism to become 'bourgeois criticism in drag', several of Showalter's contributors possess an ambivalent relation to orthodoxy. Carolyn Heilbrun presents the feminist case as a job ticket for literature teachers, 'able to combine structuralism, historical criticism, New Criticism and deconstructionism . . . to counter what threatens us: the exhaustibility of our subject'. Showalter views the rise of structuralist and post-structuralist thought as a disguised patriarchal weapon which enables 'manly, aggressive' academics to occupy themselves with form and structure, while the intuitive, expressive, feminine critics continue to work at 'humanistic' problems of content and interpretation. Later she categorizes women's culture as a 'wild zone' capable of bearing a genuinely women-centred criticism beyond the parasitic position designated by contemporary ideology.

Discussions of the canon are mainly concerned to point up texts that contain resonances for the feminist project. *Uncle Tom's Cabin*, Isak Dinesen's 'The Blank Page', Gilman's 'The Yellow Wallpaper', Susan Keating Glaspell's 'A Jury of her Peers' and a number of black and lesbian texts are the subjects of strong revisionist essays in Showalter's volume. Tinkering with the canon in this way remains a limited undertaking, a valid task, probably essential, but only in the short run. The tasks of deconstructing curricula, institutional placings and pedagogical methodology are now being inscribed in that space where we decipher the trace, 'literature'. Textuality and intertextuality, the *arrivistes* of the humanities, are not competing for the high ground; they are intent upon levelling it.

Two of the more adventurous essays here salute these issues. Susan Gubar's '"The Blank Page" and the issues of female creativity' (in Showalter) discusses the obliteration of aesthetic distance by women artists. The metaphor of pen/penis inscribing patriarchal power on the virgin page has assimilated female creativity to violation, a response to male penetration, a reaction to rending. Gubar brings the diverse arts of Isak Dinesen, Florence Nightingale, Judy Chicago and others to the task of producing a 'revisionary female theology' that appreciates the destructive power of all stereotypes. Exchanging penis for womb in the myth of creation simply perpetuates another biological imperative. As she remarks in the analysis of Dinesen's tale, 'Not to be written on is, in other words, the condition of new sorts of writing for women.' 'New sorts of writing' crystallizes the work of Rachel Blau duPlessis in 'For the Etruscans' (also in Showalter), where she creates a prose-poem of feminist discourse. DuPlessis hollows out a space that contains responsiveness to feminist philosophy, literary musings, a diary, a commonplace book and a rereading of the American literary tradition. I like it but have not yet evolved a reading practice active enough to engage in the dialogic form the essay invites.

The French writers are represented in these anthologies through commentary (original essays by Irigaray and Cixous are readily available in the indispensable *New French Feminisms*, edited by Marks and de Courtivron[1]). In these writings, the shape of a political/poetic structure/'destructure' that is responsive to a sexually situated discourse is carved out. This discourse works to undo gender subjection as part of a general project that interprets and redacts the signs of our culture, that locates the means and conditions of production of cultural artefacts including writing, that disperses the authority of meanings across peoples, histories, technologies, ideologies.

Derrida's recent 'nuclear criticism'[2] suggests the knitting together of a similar project with a considered probing of political decision. Nuclear war, he says, presents us with a 'multiplicity of dissociated heterogeneous competencies' which is 'neither coherent nor totalisable'. Military men are scientists, scientists are decision takers, decisions occur without models. Power is 'terribly accumulated, concentrated, entrusted as in a dice game to so few hands.' Avoidance of this demonic scenario depends, in Derrida's essay, upon a deconstructed account of the legend of the building of the tower of Babylon. Many languages, 'even if they didn't understand each other too well', produce an enabling rhetoric that values diversity, colloquy, continuance.

In this context, Marxist feminist criticism notes the potential occupation by women of the silences, gaps, absences and fissures in text. Derrida's use of the Babylonian prolixity, 'excess' talk, as a counter to nuclear monologism might stand here as an apt expression of the feminist cause. The strongly articulated claims of these three texts also echo Foucault's point that talking about sex is 'to pronounce a discourse that combines the fervor of knowledge, the determination to change the laws and the longing for the garden of earthly delights'.[3]

NOTES

1 Elaine Marks and Isabelle de Courtivron (eds), *New French Feminisms* (Brighton: Harvester, 1980).
2 Jacques Derrida, 'No Apocalypse, Not Now (full speed ahead, seven missiles, seven missives)', *Diacritics* (Summer 1984), pp. 20–31.
3 Paul Rabinow (ed.), *The Foucault Reader* (New York: Pantheon, 1984), pp. 295–6.

K. M. NEWTON

Textuality, teaching and theory

- Robert Scholes, *Textual Power: Literary Theory and the Teaching of English* (New Haven, Conn.: Yale University Press, 1985), 192 pp., £14.95 and £4.95

Robert Scholes has two main purposes in this book: to put forward radical proposals for altering the teaching of English in American higher education, and to attack certain contemporary theorists whose ideas would appear to undermine the theoretical assumptions underlying his proposals. In an American context Scholes's proposals certainly seem likely to be controversial, but British readers, especially those who have read the volume *Re-Reading English*, edited by Peter Widdowson (London: Methuen, 1982), may find them familiar. He believes that traditional literary study in which one concentrates on canonic works should be replaced by textual studies in which any text can be analysed:

> To put it as directly, and perhaps as brutally as possible, we must stop 'teaching literature' and start 'studying texts'.... All kinds of texts, visual as well as verbal, polemical as well as seductive, must be taken as the occasions for further textuality. And textual studies must be pushed beyond the boundaries of the page and the book into the institutional practices and social structures that can themselves be usefully studied as codes and texts. (pp. 16–17)

He proposes a tripartite scheme for the study of the text under the headings of 'reading', 'interpretation' and 'criticism'. 'Reading' involves 'a knowledge of the codes that were operative in the composition of any given text and the historical situation in which it was composed' (p. 21); 'interpretation' is founded on 'the failures of reading. It is the feeling of incompleteness on the reader's part that activates the interpretive process' (p. 22); 'criticism' involves a critique of the themes of the text or of its codes, and Scholes argues that criticism should be from the point of view of the system of values that the reader holds. The reader should not seek to subordinate his or her values to some transcendent ideal, such as literary value. That such a concept of criticism is 'extra-literary and subjects literary texts to a sort of scrutiny that is unfair, not to say vulgar, denying works their very *donnée*' is for him an advantage: 'The whole point of my argument is that we must open the way between the literary or verbal text and the social text in which we live.' The teacher of English will have to adopt a new role: 'Our job is *not* to intimidate students with our own superior textual production; it is to show them the codes upon which all textual production depends, and to encourage their own textual practice' (pp. 24–5). Scholes then goes on to show how this new approach might work in practice with a discussion of some sections of Hemingway's *In Our Time*.

The question of teaching has not been central to recent theoretical debate, but it may ultimately be the major consideration in deciding whether new theoretical perspectives will have sufficient power to end the dominance of orthodox historical and New Critical approaches. New Criticism in America was able to gain ascendancy over traditional scholarly criticism and literary impressionism because of its power in the classroom. The most powerful New Critical text was Brooks and Warren's *Understanding Poetry*, designed for the purpose of teaching poetry to students.

Can structuralist and post-structuralist theory generate teaching in English courses at the undergraduate level which will be seen as more powerful than well-established approaches? The merit of Scholes's book is to address this question and to argue that an approach based on his conception of semiotics can and should displace such established approaches. But there is a certain naïvety in his argument, since he does not discuss any resistance his proposals are likely to arouse, as if they will be considered quite disinterestedly by those who currently teach English in higher education. It seems certain that the majority of teachers will feel threatened by what Scholes proposes, since they will have neither the desire nor the capacity to change their teaching philosophy and methodology in such a drastic way. What Scholes leaves out of account in his study of textual power is the power of the institution. Many contributors to *Re-Reading English*, in contrast, believed that the changes they desired were dependent on Marxism gaining political ascendancy in the literary institution. In an American context it is difficult to envisage radical political ideas having any chance of gaining such ascendancy. One wonders, therefore, what impact his proposals will have in America, though the importance of creative writing in American courses in English may to some extent work in his favour. But one would expect Scholes's ideas to be more sympathetically received in Britain, at least in those universities and polytechnics where a more political approach to English studies has strong support. Certainly the methodology he formulates for reorienting English studies seems much more coherent and persuasive than anything suggested in *Re-Reading English*.

But, as with *Re-Reading English*, there are some difficulties he fails to consider. If 'literature' is to be discarded in favour of 'text', there can be no hierarchy of discourses. Commentary is no longer subject to the text being commented on. Deconstructionists, particularly Geoffrey Hartman, feel liberated because critics need no longer see themselves as secondary to 'creative' writers. Criticism and literature are on the same level. Scholes and many contributors to *Re-Reading English* are, however, not much interested in exploiting the 'free play' of the signifier in non-literary discourse; the emphasis is rather on exposing the underlying codes of texts. But such codes can be exposed only in terms of other codes. Scholes's version of semiotics thus runs into the problem of *Quis custodiet ipsos custodes*? Why should one ever stop exposing codes? If one abolishes textual hierarchy, there is no theoretical reason why criticism should not be infinitely regressive.

Scholes is aware that semiotics viewed as the study of codes that objectively determine the meaning of texts runs counter to Derridian deconstruction and Stanley Fish's version of reader-response criticism. Scholes proceeds to attack them. His chapter on Derrida is probably the most interesting in the book, since, by contrast with most opponents of deconstruction, he bases his attack not merely on the disastrous consequences that follow if one accepts it. Rather, he enlists such philosophical heavyweights as Peirce, Frege and Quine in order to mount an assault against Derrida's rejection of perception and the referentiality of language. His chapter on Fish is also well argued in its criticism of the concept of 'interpretive communities' and its sceptical scrutiny of some of Fish's most persuasive concrete examples.

Is Scholes right? It seems to me that deciding on this issue places the literary critic in something of a dilemma. To adopt Scholes's position on textual objectivity involves accepting certain philosophical arguments, whereas to adopt a post-structuralist position on textuality involves accepting a different set of philosophical arguments. In order to practise literary criticism of whatever kind, one must, consciously or unconsciously, make some philosophical choice. Conventional critics are often attacked by post-structuralists for their lack of theoretical engagement with the presuppositions of their critical or interpretative modes. But I think the great majority of literary critics who consider themselves to be post-structuralists would be embarrassed if they were asked whether or not they had fully taken into account the arguments of Peirce, Frege and Quine on the question of reference before concluding that Derrida was right. In deciding, do they judiciously weigh up the philosophical arguments on both sides, or do they not rather, as I suspect, allow ideological factors to determine their response?

Philosophical discourse functions as a kind of game that will go on for ever. Though everyone may be playing to win, there can be no final victory because the game never ends. Literary critics, it would seem, must nevertheless decide the winner if they are going to write any kind of critical discourse. But what does the literary critic do who is undecided whether Derrida or Quine is right? The choice this leaves one with would seem to be either to give up literary criticism or else to reconcile oneself to the fact that any decision one makes is tantamount to embracing some ideology. These considerations go beyond the scope of Scholes's book, but the fact that the book nevertheless raises them is an indication of its interest.

University of Dundee